To A

lots

fro

The Mitchell Beazley
Pocket Guide To
BIRDS
OF PREY
OF THE WORLD

MARTIN WALTERS

For Max (senior and junior)

For more detailed information on birds of prey, the following books are recommended:

Brown, L. Birds of Prey: their biology and ecology. Hamlyn 1976

Brown, L. and Amadon, D. Eagles, Hawks and Falcons of the World. Country Life 1968

Burton, P. Birds of Prey of the World. Dragon's World 1989

Clark, W. S. A Field Guide to Hawks of North America. Houghton Mifflin 1987

Cramp, S. and Simmons, K. E. L. (eds) The Birds of the Western Palearctic, Vol II. Oxford University Press 1979

Génsbøl, B. Birds of Prey of Britain and Europe. Collins 1984

Grossman, M.-L. and Hamlet, J. Birds of Prey of the World. Cassell 1965

Newton, I. (ed.) Birds of Prey. Merehurst 1990

Edited and designed by Mitchell Beazley Publishers, Michelin House, 81 Fulham Road, London SW3 6RB

Editor: Marek Walisiewicz
Art Editor: Siân Protheroe
Production: Sarah Schuman
Typesetter: Kerri Hinchon
Executive Editor: Robin Rees
Executive Art Editor: Sean Keogh

A CIP catalogue record for this book is available from the British Library

ISBN 0 85533 864 4

Although all reasonable care has been taken in the preparation of this book, neither the publishers nor the contributors or editors can accept any liability for any consequences arising from the use thereof or from the information contained herein.

Typeset in Sabon
Linotronic output by The Imaging Business, London N7
Reproduced by Mandarin Offset, Hong Kong
Produced by Mandarin Offset, Hong Kong

Contents

Introduction

Birds of prey (or raptors) have always been a source of fascination and, perhaps more than any other group of birds, they engender feelings of awe and respect. They can be seen in nearly all parts of the world, and in a wide range of habitats, from dense tropical forests to open plains and deserts. Some, such as the European Kestrel and the Black Kite, are common even in urban areas or alongside major roads. Others, for example many of the true eagles, inhabit lonely, mountainous country and are hard to approach.

Wherever they occur, birds of prey are exciting to watch; their feeding methods are spectacular, and many indulge in elaborate aerobatic displays during the breeding season. Their presence in a habitat is often the sign of a balanced ecosystem, since they mostly feed upon live animals, which are themselves dependent upon a healthy environment. Their conservation therefore goes hand in hand with the preservation of a wide range of other animals and plants.

Of the 9,300 species of birds recognized today, about 295 (depending on the exact system of classification followed) are considered to be birds of prey. They fall into five families, which together make up the Falconiformes, one of the 28 avian orders. Within this broad classification, 18 distinct groups are recognized. This book gives a brief introduction to the biology of these magnificent birds, followed by a group-by-group account of all existing species.

The biology of birds of prey

Feeding strategies

All birds of prey have hooked beaks, which are often deep and powerful, strong feet equipped with sharp claws, and relatively large eyes. These basic features enable them to kill, seize and feed upon other animals, ranging from small insects to large mammals and birds. Most birds of prey capture live animals, but some feed either wholly or partly on carrion.

Vultures have long, flexible necks with short, downy feathers, and areas of bare flesh on their faces. This helps them extract flesh from carcases without getting soiled in the process. With their heavy, hooked bills they tear open the thick skin of freshly killed antelopes and other large mammals. Three vulture species, the widespread Turkey Vulture, and the two yellow-headed vultures, hunt partly by smell, and can detect a hidden carcase, even distinguishing between fresh and rotten meat, using scent alone. Other vultures rely upon sight to home in on dead animals, or to detect the activities of other predators, including other vultures, and follow them to a kill. Vultures spend many hours prospecting for food in energy-efficient soaring flight. Their long, broad wings help them take advantage of rising air masses to gain height. Griffon vultures look for food in search parties; when any one of the group spots a possible meal, the others quickly follow.

The Osprey and fish eagles have long, sharp, strongly curved claws and tiny spikes under their toes, to help them grasp and hang on to their slippery prey. Kites, especially Brahminy and Black Kites, also occasionally take fish from the water surface, but their feet are less specialized for this purpose. Most kites are generalist feeders, scavenging for small mammals, birds and reptiles, but also taking invertebrates. They are acrobatic in the air, often changing direction rapidly to swoop down suddenly on to their food. The smaller kites are delicate, almost tern-like in behaviour, and hunt by hovering, or chase small prey in mid-air.

Snake eagles, as their name implies, specialize in snakes, although most species take a wide range of reptiles and other vertebrate prey as well. They have short, sturdy legs and toes, well protected by scales or feathers. Their flat faces and large, forward-facing eyes, give them the good binocular vision needed for spotting well-camouflaged prey.

Harriers hunt by gliding low over rough country, such as marsh or meadow, gazing intently at the ground below, watching mainly for small mammals, or birds. They are light in build and can quickly turn and drop down on to their prey, using their long legs to grasp it from amongst the grass or reed stems.

Buzzards and eagles are adapted to hunting mammals, varying in size from small voles and mice, to small deer, monkeys and antelopes. Falcons and *Accipiters* are streamlined for the rapid pursuit of aerial prey – usually other birds. Their eyesight is particularly keen and they are capable of rapid acceleration when chasing their quarry. Their long legs, slender toes and sharp claws help them grasp and hold on to their prey, while their strongly-hooked bills enable them to subdue it quickly, usually with a fatal bite to the neck. The sturdy bill is also a help in plucking the feathers from captured birds. In general, falcons feed in much more open habitats than *Accipiters*. Their wings tend to be long and pointed as an adaptation to rapid, direct flight. In contrast, the wings of *Accipiters* tend to be relatively short and rounded to help them pursue their prey between the trunks and branches of forest trees.

The caracaras are generalist and opportunist feeders. They are equipped with sharply hooked bills, and can catch and kill their own prey, often the helpless young of other birds, or invertebrates. However, they take a good deal of carrion as well, and have bare skin on their faces.

Breeding

The majority of birds of prey breed in solitary pairs. However, around 15% of species (including many kites) are colonial nesters. Most are monogamous, that is the breeding unit consists of one male and one female, and moreover, the pair may remain faithful to each other for several seasons. There are some interesting exceptions; the Galápagos Hawk, for example, is polyandrous, each female pairing up with two or more males. The opposite arrangement, polygyny, is seen in some harriers. A successful male harrier may support two or more females at different nests within his territory. Male Hen Harriers have been recorded with as many as six females in such a harem.

Most raptors build nests, usually from sticks or twigs woven together. The most impressive are the huge eyries built by Golden and Bald Eagles, which are often used for many years in succession and added to each season. The New World vultures and the falcons, however, build no nest at all. They lay their eggs in a simple scrape or hollow, or take over the existing nest of another bird.

Elaborate courtship displays early in the breeding season are a particular feature of some birds of prey. In certain groups, notably the eagles, harriers and kites, such displays involve complicated and acrobatic flights over the nesting area. In these flights, the male bird often appears to attack the female in a dive or stoop, whereupon the female turns over and the two grapple talons, sometimes plunging

The male Marsh Harrier transfers food morsels to the female as part of an elaborate courtship ritual, and also during incubation, when the female spends most of her time on the nest

towards the ground before separating again. In harriers, these displays may include the mid-air transfer of food from one sex to the other.

Threats to birds of prey

Birds of prey have long suffered the consequences of human activity. In many parts of the world the larger species are regarded by farmers and gamekeepers as a threat to livestock, and are trapped inhumanely, or poisoned illegally. These practices continue even in those countries with strict conservation laws and a high public awareness of wildlife. While it is true that some of the larger eagles and hawks occasionally take farmed livestock, such losses seldom have any direct effect on farmers' livelihoods, and usually only dead or sick animals are attacked.

The extensive use of agrochemicals over the last few decades has disrupted many finely balanced ecosystems. Birds of prey are particularly susceptible to the effects of these chemicals since they are at the pinnacle of their food chains, and therefore rapidly concentrate toxins in their bodies. In the 1960s and 1970s, chlorinated hydrocarbons, such as DDT, were widely used as seed dressings and pesticides. These compounds persist in the environment for many years, and can either kill birds outright, or accumulate in their bodies, disrupting their reproduction by reducing the thickness of their eggshells. Eggs with thinner than normal shells usually fail to develop, and so the species fails to reproduce. Sparrowhawks and Peregrines were particulary affected by this problem, but there is now evidence of a slow recovery in those areas where use of these chemicals is restricted.

Wild populations of certain species have been reduced by the activities of egg-collectors, and by the demand for birds for falconry. The larger falcons and some hawks, such as the goshawks, are sought after by falconers, commanding high prices, particularly in the Arab world. There have been many thefts, either of eggs or of young birds, to supply this trade, mostly affecting the Peregrine, Gyr Falcon, Saker and the already vulnerable Lanner.

The major threat to birds of prey undoubtedly comes from the direct destruction or alteration of their habitats. Agriculture and other human pressures continue to remove natural and near-natural bird habitats, and there is usually a decline in raptor populations as an area becomes more intensively settled or cultivated. Wetlands and tropical forests have come under particularly severe threat in recent years, and unsurprisingly these habitats contain many of the rarest raptor species, such as the Madagascar and Kinabalu Serpent Eagles, the *Leucopternis* hawks, the solitary eagles, the Javan Hawk Eagle, Guiana Crested Eagle, Harpy Eagle, New Guinea Harpy Eagle, Philippine Eagle, and the tiny forest falcons. Worst hit are species that prey on large animals, which themselves require large, undisturbed territories, and those birds with a limited distribution, such as island endemics.

Habitat change does not always ring the death knell for birds of prey. The highly adaptable Black Kite and American Black Vulture have thrived near human settlements; and in California, the White-tailed Kite has increased in cultivated areas.

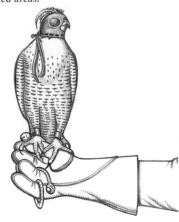

The Peregrine is much sought after by falconers since it is one of the easiest raptors to train. These birds are quite capable of killing animals larger than themselves, though pigeons, ducks and waders are their favoured prey in the wild

About the book

All the world's birds of prey are described and illustrated in this book. Each species is assigned to one of 18 major groups, the members of which share certain physical and behavioural characteristics. A general introduction highlights the features that typify each group, and gives an account of favoured habitats and prey. The larger groups (such as the buzzards and their relatives) are rather heterogeneous: in these cases, the introduction surveys the subdivisions of the group. Three species (the Secretary Bird, Osprey and Laughing Falcon) have no close relatives and are classified in their own groups, for which introductions are not necessary.

Within each group, closely related species appear on adjacent pages. The species entries give details of distribution, preferred habitat, and status. The names of endangered species are underlined in the captions. Information on the breeding biology of individual species is not included, partly because of constraints upon space, but also because many birds have not been studied in sufficient depth for reliable data to be available. Throughout the book, birds are shown in full adult plumage unless otherwise indicated. Plumage differences between the sexes, or between adult and immature birds, are illustrated when they occur. To aid identification in the field, most species are pictured in flight, as well as perched.

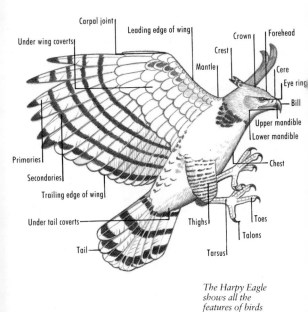

The Harpy Eagle shows all the features of birds of prey referred to in the book

Family Cathartidae. 7 species in 5 genera

The bare skin on this King Vulture's face helps it keep clean. The variable colour and pattern on this skin also enables individuals to recognize each other

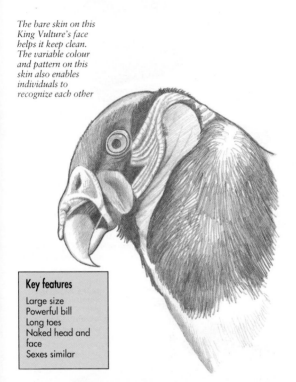

Key features

Large size
Powerful bill
Long toes
Naked head and face
Sexes similar

The New World vultures are all large to very large birds. Most have brown or dark plumage, and the sexes are difficult to distinguish in the field. They seldom kill their own prey, but are well adapted to a diet of carrion and refuse. Most have bare skin around the head and neck, which allows them to feed inside a carcase without matting down their feathers. With excellent vision, they can spot food rapidly in forests as well as in open terrain; moreover, members of the genus *Cathartes* such as the Turkey Vulture, have a keen sense of smell that helps them locate food, even when out of sight. These vultures frequently soar for long periods on rising air masses, scouring the country below for signs of food, such as groups of other birds of prey.

The New World vultures breed slowly, laying just one or two eggs per year (or in the case of the condors, a single egg every other year), which are incubated for between five and eight weeks. Although members of this family are superficially similar to the Old World vultures and play a comparable role in nature, the two groups of birds are not closely related; indeed some scientists regard the New World vulures as having closer links with storks.

New World vultures

Andean Condor
Status: *Widespread*
Length: *116 cm*
Wingspan: *280 cm*
*Plumage glossy black
with white wing
patches and a white
ruff of down around
the neck*

The **Andean Condor** *Vultur gryphus* is the largest of all birds of prey and, at up to 14 kg in weight, also one of the heaviest flying birds. Its distribution largely follows the Andes down western South America, from Colombia and Venezuela to Chile and Argentina. These condors usually nest on rocky ledges around 3,000 to 4,500 m up. Although widespread, they are by no means common, and are often killed by livestock farmers.

California Condor
Status: *Extinct (in wild)*
Length: *117 cm*
Wingspan: *275 cm*

*Triangular white
patches on undersides
of wings in flight.
Plumage dark grey-
brown, with white
under wing coverts.
Head, neck and crop
area bare*

The **California Condor** *Gymnogyps californianus* is the North American counterpart of the Andean Condor. It is now extinct in the wild but had its final stronghold in California. The last wild bird was taken into captivity in 1987 to join a captive breeding and re-introduction programme. There is plenty of suitable habitat available, but since condors only breed every other year, re-introduction is likely to be a very slow process.

Turkey Vulture
Status: *Common*
Length: *70 cm*
Wingspan: *175 cm*
Glides with wings held in a shallow V. In flight, long tail extends beyond legs

Pale flight feathers contrast with darker body and wing coverts

The Turkey Vulture *Cathartes aura* has a range that stretches from southern Canada to Tierra del Fuego, taking in the islands of the Caribbean and the Falklands. Common in the dry, open country and farmland of North America, where they are often called "buzzards", Turkey Vultures take carrion, fruit and vegetables, and sometimes scavenge along the tideline. With their keen sense of smell, they are often the first birds to arrive at a carcase.

Black Vulture
Status: *Locally common*
Length: *65 cm*
Wingspan: *150 cm*
Pale patches at base of primaries are prominent in flight

The Black Vulture *Coragyps atratus* is a compact, black bird found in southern and eastern USA and most of South America, though it is absent from southern Chile and Argentina. It often feeds with Turkey Vultures where their ranges overlap and usually displaces these larger birds when quarrelling over food. Black Vultures are frequently seen scavenging at rubbish dumps and fisheries. These short-tailed vultures fly with wings held nearly flat.

King Vulture
Status: *Locally common*
Length: *76 cm*
Wingspan: *162 cm*

Strange, gaudy face colouration, white staring eye with red ring. Heavy bill

The **King Vulture** *Sarcoramphus papa* is heavier than the Turkey Vulture, with broader, condor-like wings. It lives mostly in the dense tropical forests of Central and South America (particularly Amazonia) where it hunts by soaring high above the trees or over adjacent grassy areas and rivers. High in the pecking order at a carcase.

Yellow-headed Vulture
Status: *Local*
Length: *80 cm*
Wingspan: *162 cm*
(Left) Blue-grey crown, red cere

Gtr. Yellow-headed Vulture
Status: *Uncertain*
Length: *85 cm*
Wingspan: *166 cm*
(Right) Yellow head with blue crown

The **Yellow-headed (Savanna) Vulture** *Cathartes burrovianus* lives in Mexico, Panama, and the northern half of South America, east of the Andes; the **Greater Yellow-headed (Wetmore Forest) Vulture** *Cathartes melambrotus* is found scattered throughout Amazonia. Both of these vultures are close relatives of the smaller, more common Turkey Vulture.

Secretary Bird

Family Sagittariidae. 1 species in 1 genus

Secretary Bird
Status: *Widespread, but rather uncommon and decreasing*
Length: *150 cm*
Wingspan: *210 cm*
Long legs, elongated central tail feathers, distinctive crest

The Secretary Bird *Sagittarius serpentarius* has no close relatives and is therefore classified in its own family. It is the least "raptor-like" of all birds of prey, and in many ways resembles a stork or crane. Its long legs are an adaptation to stalking prey (mainly reptiles, rodents and insects) in tall grass. The bird paces slowly through the grass, occasionally lunging down to stamp on its prey, or seize it in its sharp bill. This species of dry grassland and savanna is found in Africa south of the Sahara. It builds huge nests of twigs, often at the tops of *Acacia* trees. Although they hunt mostly on the ground, Secretary Birds are graceful in flight, using their broad wings to take advantage of rising air currents. They sometimes soar to great heights over their breeding grounds, uttering odd groaning calls.

The Secretary Bird's name comes from the feathers on its crest, which resemble the old-fashioned quill pens once used by lawyers' clerks.

13

Osprey

Family Pandionidae. 1 species in 1 genus

Osprey
Status: *Locally common*
Length: *55-60 cm*
Wingspan: *145-170 cm*
Sexes differ only slightly in plumage

The Osprey's wings are angled in flight. Wings mainly white below, with dark patches at the carpal joint. The bird is usually seen over water

The Osprey pulls in its wings as it enters the water, its talons stretched to the full

The Osprey (Fish Hawk) *Pandion haliaetus* is classified in a family of its own. Easily identified by its brown and white plumage and long, angled wings, this hawk-like bird is found worldwide, sharing with the Peregrine the widest distribution of any bird of prey.

Ospreys feed almost entirely on fish and are well adapted to their specialist diet. They hunt by diving feet first into the water with half closed wings, emerging with their prey grasped in their talons. Rough surfaces on the undersides of their toes give secure purchase on their slippery quarry. Ospreys usually nest in trees near the coast or freshwater lakes, but are also at home in artificial nest sites, such as specially-constructed poles or platforms.

Cuckoo falcons

Family Accipitridae (part). 5 species in 1 genus

This Crested Baza shows the typical yellow eye, crest and notched bill of the cuckoo falcons. The plumage patterns, particularly when in flight, can be reminiscent of a cockatoo

Key features

Double-notched
upper mandible
Crest
Sexes differ

These small kite-relatives live in forest and scrub in Africa, south and east Asia, with one species reaching north-east Australia. Baza is the name usually given to the Asian and Australian species, whilst the African residents are normally known as cuckoo falcons. All have a crest at the back of the head, which varies in length according to the species. Members of the family display a distinctive wide-barred pattern on their undersides, and have a parrot-like notched upper mandible, which helps them to kill small vertebrates quickly, but may also be an adaptation to feeding on fruit.

Cuckoo falcons are mainly forest birds. Their diet comprises insects and small vertebrates, such as frogs, reptiles and birds. When hunting, they frequently scramble about amongst the branches in pusuit of their prey, or in search of tropical fruits, such as figs. There is some evidence that they are active during the evening, as well as by day. They are sociable birds and often gather in groups of 20 or more, especially outside the breeding season.

Early in the breeding season, cuckoo falcons display to each other in active aerial chases, often accompanied by whistling calls. They build small, rather fragile twig nests high in the tree tops. Each year they lay two to five eggs, which are incubated by both sexes for four to five weeks.

Cuckoo falcons

Crested Baza
Status: *Widespread*
Length: *35-46 cm*
Wingspan: *80-110 cm*
*Dark crest, bright
yellow eye. Under-tail
coverts amber-brown*

African Cuckoo Falcon
Status: *Local*
Length: *43 cm*
Wingspan: *100 cm*
*Underside of wings
rufous*

The Crested Baza *Aviceda subcristata* is known variously as the Crested Hawk, Pacific Baza and the Pacific Cuckoo Falcon. This relatively tame bird is found in New Guinea, Maluku (the Moluccas), south-west Pacific islands, and coastal northern and north-east Australia. It hunts in tropical forests and along woodland margins, mainly for insects, small amphibians and reptiles, but will also take fruit. These birds are often seen in groups outside the breeding season.

The African Cuckoo Falcon (African Cuckoo Hawk) *Aviceda cuculoides* lives in Africa south of the Sahara. This forest hawk feeds mostly on insects, reptiles and small birds. It has heavy, rather slow wingbeats and shows rufous barring on the belly.

16

Jerdon's Baza
Status: *Locally common*
Length: *46 cm*
Wingspan: *110 cm*
Brown plumage with black stripe on throat. Rufous breast

Black Baza
Status: *Locally common*
Length: *33 cm*
Wingspan: *79 cm*
Mostly black plumage, with white breast band and wing patches. Crest longer than other bazas

Madagascar Cuckoo Falcon
Status: *Local/narrow endemic*
Length: *40 cm*
Wingspan: *96 cm*
Brown plumage

Jerdon's Baza (Asian Baza) *Aviceda jerdoni* is widespead in Sri Lanka, Sikkim, Burma, Hainan, Sumatra, Borneo, Sulawesi and the Philippines, notably in hill forests, but also in tea plantations. It is particularly active around dawn and dusk.

The Black Baza *Aviceda leuphotes* lives in the Himalayan foothills, South China and Hainan, migrating to India and South-east Asia in the winter. With its slow-flapping flight and dark plumage, this species is somewhat reminiscent of a crow. Black Bazas are relatively tame birds and are often seen in pairs or small flocks.

The Madagascar Cuckoo Falcon (Madagascar Cuckoo Hawk) *Aviceda madagascariensis* is restricted to the forests of Madagascar.

Kites, honey buzzards and relatives

Family Accipitridae (part). 27 species in 16 genera

This group comprises five species of honey buzzards, 21 species of kites and the rather mysterious Bat Hawk. All are medium-sized to large birds, whose sexes are similar in appearance. They vary in plumage both between, and in a few cases, within species.

The fine-pointed bill of the Slender-billed Kite (below) allows it to extract snails from their shells

Key features

Slim, elegant build
Long tail
Small head
Sturdy feet
Stiff hairs on face
Sexes similar

Honey buzzards are similar in build to the large hawks and true buzzards, though they are slimmer and have longer tails. The small, rather pigeon-like head is held well forward on a long neck. These raptors inhabit forests and woodlands, and are adapted to take advantage of a food little exploited by other birds of prey - the combs, grubs and adults of bees and wasps - although most also eat other insects and small vertebrates. Honey buzzards use their sturdy feet to dig out the combs from wasp and bee nests, and their bills to remove the stings from the adult insects. The face is protected from stings by its close covering of short, rather stiff feathers.

Honey buzzards are strongly migratory in the northern parts of their range. They move south in the autumn and north again in the spring, crossing in enormous numbers over Gibraltar and the Bosphorus. They usually lay two eggs, which hatch after about 32 days.

The head of the Western Honey Buzzard (below) is densely feathered, as protection against stings

Bill shape varies according to diet. The Red Kite (above) is a generalist feeder

*The deep, heavy bill
of this Hook-billed
Kite helps it feed on
snails, reptiles, birds
and insects*

Kites also have long tails, which are distinctly notched or forked in
most species. The tail is very flexible, and can be twisted easily from
side to side, acting as a rudder to direct flight. The notch is thought to
give even finer control of movement. These birds display variations on
the basic raptor hooked bill according to the different kinds of food
taken. The generalist feeders, such as the Red and Black Kites, have
medium-sized bills with modestly hooked tips, while the partly
insectivorous *Elanus* kites have small bills and large gapes. The bizarre
deeply-hooked bills of the Snail, Slender-billed and Hook-billed Kites
are an adaptation to dealing with their mollusc prey.

Six of the kites are bulky and predominantly brown in colour. Of
these, the Black Kite is the most common. This cosmopolitan bird has
thrived partly because it has learned to exploit the ecological niches
opened up by a growing human population. Most of the remaining 15
species are smaller, paler, and more delicate birds. They feed mostly in
or from the air, and are the most acrobatic of all raptors. They are
buoyant and graceful in flight, flapping slowly and gliding with their
wings angled backwards.

Some kites, particularly the swallow-tailed kites and the Letter-
winged Kite, are social breeders, building their nests together in loose
colonies. These species also hunt in groups or flocks, following each
other to take advantage of locally-abundant food, such as insect
swarms. Others, such as the Black, Brahminy and Whistling Kites,
although not breeding socially, gather together when feeding on
carrion and refuse.

Kites build their nests in trees and often decorate them with brightly
coloured material.

*The upper mandible
of the Bat Hawk is
unique in being
keeled. This feature,
together with the very
wide gape, enables
the bird to grasp
flying bats and
swallow them whole*

The Bat Hawk is normally classified along with the kites, though it is
so odd that it probably has no close relatives. Its head, large eye and
crest are kite-like, but it has a falcon's long, pointed wings and a bill
more reminiscent of a Nightjar. The toes, like those of many falcons,
have raised bumps beneath to help grasp struggling prey.

Honey buzzards

Western Honey Buzzard
Status: *Local*
Length: *52-60 cm*
Wingspan: *135-150 cm*

Barring under tail and wings. Long, pigeon-like head. Yellow legs and eyes. Immature bird in flight, top right

The immature Westen Honey Buzzard (left) can be distinguished from the adult by its dark eyes

Eastern Honey Buzzard
Status: *Local*
Length: *69 cm*
Wingspan: *170 cm*
(Below and right)
Black chin stripe

The **(Western) Honey Buzzard** *Pernis apivorus* is more closely related to the kites than to the true buzzards. A bird of woodland, it is found throughout most of Europe, to western Siberia. In Europe, the largest populations are in Sweden and France. Honey Buzzards have a varied diet, feeding on larvae, pupae and adults of bees, wasps and ants, as well as on other insects, mammals and reptiles. Northern birds spend the winters in Africa and large migrating flocks are often seen at sea crossings such as in south Sweden, Gibraltar and the Bosphorus.

The **Eastern Honey Buzzard** *Pernis ptilorhynchus* replaces its western relative in eastern Siberia, China and Japan, and is also found in India and South-East Asia. Both species are variable in plumage.

Long-tailed Honey Buzzard
Status: *Local/narrow endemic*
Length: *53 cm*
Wingspan: *140 cm*
Long tail

Black Honey Buzzard
Status: *Rare/narrow endemic*
Length: *53 cm*
Wingspan: *140 cm*
Striking black and white plumage

Barred Honey Buzzard
Status: *Local*
Length: *55 cm*
Wingspan: *145 cm*
Short crest, heavily barred underparts. Plumage mimics that of Sulawesi Hawk-Eagle

The **Long-tailed Honey Buzzard** *Henicopernis longicauda* is a native of New Guinea. It nests in the forest but hunts low over adjacent cultivated areas, in the manner of a harrier.

The closely related **Black Honey Buzzard** *Henicopernis infuscata* is restricted to the Pacific island of New Britain, where it lives along the rainforest margins. Its habitat is threatened by logging and this bird is now rarely seen. This species is remarkably similar in plumage to the Sulawesi Hawk Eagle (p. 149), and overlaps with it in range.

The **Barred Honey Buzzard** *Pernis celebensis* lives in Indonesia, the Philippines and Sulawesi. Populations in the Philippines have paler plumage, with yellow-brown replacing dark brown above.

21

Small kites

American Swallow-tailed Kite
Status: *Local*
Length: *58 cm*
Wingspan: *122 cm*
*Tail deeply forked
with bold black and
white pattern below*

Pearl Kite
Status: *Local*
Length: *22 cm*
Wingspan: *60 cm*
*Falcon-like head, tail
and wings. Mainly
white below*

African Swallow-tailed Kite
Status: *Local*
Length: *36 cm*
Wingspan: *75 cm*

*Pale grey above,
white below with
black patch at angle
of wing. Deeply
forked tail*

The **American Swallow-tailed Kite** *Elanoides forficatus* is probably the world's most graceful bird of prey. It lives in swampy habitats from northern Argentina through to the southern USA (especially Florida) and is often seen in small flocks. It feeds entirely in the air, mostly on insects, but also on young birds and reptiles.

The **Pearl Kite** *Gampsonyx swainsonii* is a small kite of the South American savanna which resembles the falconets. It hunts from tree branches for small insects.

The **African Swallow-tailed** (Scissor-tailed) Kite *Chelictinia riocourii* is a dainty, elegant bird of the dry savannas and semi-deserts at the southern edge of the Sahara. Like its relatives the *Elanus* kites, it frequently hovers and often hunts in small parties.

Black-shouldered Kite
Status: *Local*
Length: *33 cm*
Wingspan: *86 cm*
*Slim, falcon-like build
and pale plumage.
Bright red eye*

White-tailed Kite
Status: *Locally
common*
Length: *41 cm*
Wingspan: *107 cm*
*Distinctive black
carpal patches under
wings*

The **Black-shouldered Kite** *Elanus caeruleus* is distributed widely throughout southern, eastern and central Africa, India and South-East Asia. The species is scattered in northern Africa and also present in Spain and Portugal, where populations are increasing. It feeds on small mammals, birds, reptiles and insects.

Its American counterpart, the slightly larger White-tailed Kite *Elanus leucurus,* is very similar in build, plumage and habit. It lives mainly in South and Central America and is increasing in southern and western USA, especially west California, south Texas and along the Gulf coast. It eats mostly small mammals such as mice. Both species hover when hunting and often settle on telegraph poles or wires. They are sociable, often seen in small groups.

Small kites

Australian Black-shouldered Kite
Status: *Locally common*
Length: *33-38 cm*
Wingspan: *90 cm*
Dark carpal patches like White-tailed Kite, but primaries darker

Letter-winged Kite
Status: *Locally common*
Length: *35-38 cm*
Wingspan: *90 cm*
Large, owl-like head with large eyes. Distinctive "letter" marks beneath wings

The Australian Black-shouldered Kite *Elanus notatus*, also known as the Black-winged Kite, is found in open forest and grassland throughout mainland Australia.

The **Letter-winged Kite** *Elanus scriptus* takes its name from the unusual markings on the undersides of its wings. It is the only truly nocturnal bird of prey, emerging at dusk to feed on its main prey, the Long-haired Rat (*Rattus villosissimus*) and other rodents. It is a very sociable bird and flocks of 50-100 individuals are often seen roosting in trees (especially coolabah trees). It lives in the plains of inland Australia, where its preferred habitat is open grassland with scattered trees and watercourses.

Snail Kite
Status: *Locally common*
Length: *43 cm*
Wingspan: *117 cm*
Red eye and deeply hooked bill. Female and juvenile have quite different plumage from adult male

Slender-billed Kite
Status: *Uncommon*
Length: *38 cm*
Wingspan: *110 cm*
Yellow eye. Wings and tail shorter than Snail Kite

The **Snail Kite (Everglade Kite)** *Rostrhamus sociabilis* is widespread and often common in Central and South America, especially in the marshland of northern Argentina. The species is also found in the Florida Everglades, where it is rather local and restricted to the marshes. Snail Kites feed almost exclusively on freshwater snails of the genus *Pomacea*, which they pluck from the water surface with their feet. They fly low over the water, sometimes in large groups.

The Slender-billed Kite *Rostrhamus hamatus* is found only in northern South America. Like its more cosmopolitan relative, it feeds mainly on *Pomacea* snails. Both species have specially adapted bills to enable them to extract the snails from their shells.

Mississippi Kite
Status: *Local*
Length: *37 cm*
Wingspan: *89 cm*
*Grey plumage, black
forked tail*

Plumbeous Kite
Status: *Locally
common*
Length: *35 cm*
Wingspan: *85 cm*
*White markings on
unforked tail*

The Mississippi Kite *Ictinia mississippiensis* is a grey falcon-like bird that is increasing its range in the southern USA. Its breeding range centres on the southern Great Plains, extending into the Mississippi valley to southern Illinois and in an arc from the Gulf coast through northern Florida to North Carolina. This raptor is buoyant in flight, often soaring for long periods on its flat wings.

The **Plumbeous Kite** *Ictinia plumbea* has a wider range in Central and South America. These birds are often seen in flocks, sometimes together with Swallow-tailed Kites (p.22). Their favoured method of hunting is to soar and swoop on flying insects, catching larger prey (such as reptiles) in their talons.

Hook-billed Kite
Status: *Local/local and local and rare (USA)*
Length: *40 cm*
Wingspan: *85 cm*
White eyes, large hooked bill and rounded wings

The male bird (perched above and in flight) can be distinguished from the female by its grey-barred underparts and grey head

Cayenne Kite
Status: *Local*
Length: *45 cm*
Wingspan: *95 cm*
Black and white plumage. Large dark eyes

The Hook-billed Kite *Chondrohierax uncinatus* lives in dense forest in Central America and northern South America, where it feeds on snails, amphibians and insects. There are also about 20 breeding pairs in South Texas. This sociable kite often gathers in flocks of 20 or more. The rare Cuban form is sometimes considered to be a separate species (*Chondrohierax wilsonii*).

The Cayenne Kite (Grey-headed Kite) *Leptodon cayanensis* includes wasp larvae and wasps' nests in its diet. It is a bird of tropical forest areas (favouring streams and marshes), from Mexico to Argentina and Paraguay. It can sometimes be spotted soaring over the forest, showing its distinctive long, rounded wings and tail.

27

Small kites

Double-toothed Kite
Status: *Local*
Length: *33 cm*
Wingspan: *70 cm*
Male barred below, female barred only on belly. Note the notched upper mandible, black throat stripe and large orange eye

Rufous-thighed Kite
Status: *Local*
Length: *33 cm*
Wingspan: *70 cm*
Light grey below with orange-red "trousers". Note the notched upper mandible and part-feathered legs

The **Double-toothed Kite** *Harpagus bidentatus* takes its name from its distinctive two-notched upper mandible. Present from southern Mexico to Bolivia, it preys on small lizards and insects, which it takes from the branches of trees. Its flight incorporates hawk-like glides.

The **Rufous-thighed Kite** *Harpagus diodon* is a little studied species, restricted to the eastern part of tropical South America.

The hawk (*Accipiter*)-like shape of these two kites enables them to fly quickly and with great manoeverability among the trees of their forest habitat. The notched upper mandible is a feature shared by the Cuckoo Falcons (pp. 15-17), which also forage amongst tree branches for their insect and reptile prey.

Black Kite
Status: *Common*
Length: *55-60 cm*
Wingspan: *170 cm*
Resembles a dark buzzard in flight, but is more agile and flaps more frequently

In flight, the Black Kite's plumage appears uniformly dark, although young birds have pale wing patches. The notched tail is not always clear when soaring

The Black Kite *Milvus migrans* is one of the world's most successful raptors. It is widespread in Europe, Australia (where it is commonly known as the Fork-tailed Kite), Africa (Yellow-billed Kite) and Asia (Pariah Kite). It is often associated with human habitations.

Black Kites feed on a very wide range of animals, and will also take refuse and carrion, particularly fish. They are sociable and very vocal, uttering shrill, juddering squeals, and are frequently seen cruising and sailing over water on the lookout for dead fish. European residents begin the annual migration to their winter quarters in Africa as early as July and are often seen in large numbers over narrow sea crossings. Most make the return journey in March or April.

29

Red Kite

Status: *Local, declining*
Length: *60-66 cm*
Wingspan: *175-195 cm*
Rich chestnut plumage with pale head, white wing patches and russet tail

The Red Kite's long, deeply forked tail and angled wings are visible in flight. In flight, the immature bird (left) shows paler plumage than the adult (right)

The Red Kite *Milvus milvus,* like the Black Kite, is a large, buzzard-shaped bird: it can be distinguished from its relative by its deeply forked tail. The Red Kite's stronghold is Europe (especially Germany and Spain), but populations have declined markedly in recent years. A small, isolated population in mid-Wales is slowly building up. In contrast to the very widespread black Kite, the Red Kite is restricted almost entirely to Europe, where it breeds in wooded habitats, usually nesting in a tall oak, beech or coniferous tree.

Some of the northern populations migrate to Africa in the autumn, but others, such as those in Wales and Sweden, may remain throughout the season, especially in mild winters.

This agile and graceful bird likes to hunt in hilly country with mixed forest, pasture, cultivated land and fish-rich lakes. It is also commonly seen scavenging at rubbish tips or patrolling roads on the lookout for animals killed by passing traffic.

Brahminy Kite
Status: *Locally common*
Length: *48 cm*
Wingspan: *145 cm*
Adult birds (below and perched above) have rich chestnut and white plumage. Immatures are brown and streaked below

The Brahminy Kite *Haliastur indus* is a powerful, acrobatic bird found around shores, estuaries and rice paddies in India, Sri Lanka, Indonesia and northern Australia. It preys mainly on small vertebrates (including fish), crabs and carrion, but will also take food such as winged termites in mid-air. In certain areas, notably India, it is a common scavenger near settlements and harbours, and along the tide line.

Brahminy Kites have a slow, soaring flight, and rounded wings and tail. They are normally seen singly, in pairs or in small groups and build their stick nests high in trees, often near to water.

Like many other birds of prey, Brahminy Kites tend to line their nests with green twigs, and, like several other kites, they also include pieces of paper and cloth in the nest, giving it a rather untidy look. The female does most of the incubation of the eggs and is fed by the male during this period, until the young hatch, after an incubation period of around four weeks.

Large kites

Black-breasted Kite
Status: *Scarce*
Length: *53-60 cm*
Wingspan: *150 cm*
Dark chest and back, with rufous neck and thighs. In flight, white "window" in black wingtips and short, rounded tail are visible

Black-breasted Kite occurs in dark (above) and pale (left) phases. Pale phase has buff plumage, mottled on the back

Whistling Kite
Status: *Common*
Length: *50-58 cm*
Wingspan: *120 cm*
Long, rounded tail and white wing-patches

The **Black-breasted Kite** (**Black-breasted Buzzard Kite**) *Hamirostra melanosternon* is perhaps the least typical of the kites, more closely resembling a buzzard or small eagle. This Australian species adopts a rocking motion as it glides, calling to mind the Bateleur of Africa (see p. 56). Its diet consists mainly of reptiles, small mammals such as rabbits, and eggs.

The **Whistling Kite** *Haliastur sphenurus* is one of Australia's commonest birds of prey: it is also found on Papua New Guinea. It prefers forested hills, estuaries, lakes, and wooded river valleys and takes live prey such as small mammals, reptiles and birds, but also gathers in groups to feed on carrion.

Square-tailed Kite
Status: *Local/rare*
Length: *50-56 cm*
Wingspan: *120 cm*
Pale head has slight crest. Wings extend beyond tail when perched

Note long, broad wings, and pale patches at the base of primaries

The Square-tailed Kite *Lophoictinia isura* is an Australian raptor with long, upswept wings and a harrier-like flight. It is a bird of open woodland and rocky gorges, but tends to avoid the dry inland plains, closed forest and agricultural areas. The distribution of this species is patchy: it is most often seen in north and west Australia (Arnhem Land and Kimberley), and along the Great Dividing Range in Queensland.

It feeds mainly on live prey such as small birds, reptiles and insects, and is less of a scavenger than most other large kites. It sometimes hunts by quartering over open country, in the manner of a harrier, but usually at greater height and speed.

Bat Hawk

Bat Hawk
Status: *Local*
Length: *45 cm*
Wingspan: *125 cm*
Large eye, large feet and keeled upper mandible.

The Bat Hawk is powerful and falcon-like in flight, when its square-cut tail and long, pointed wings are visible

The Bat Hawk (Bat Kite) *Machaerhamphus alcinus* is one of the most unusual of all birds of prey. This native of tropical Africa, Madagascar, Malaya and Indonesia is only active for short periods around dawn and dusk when it feeds voraciously on bats – its main prey – as well as swallows, swiftlets and insects. During the day it remains hidden in foliage.

The Bat Hawk is well adapted to its way of life with wide eyes to help it to see clearly in dim light, powerful talons to help it grab bats in mid-air and a wide, Nightjar-like gape to enable it to swallow prey whole while still in flight. Bat Hawks are particularly common near entrances to bat caves, but also occur in towns and along rivers. Unless observed at their feeding sites, however, they are not easy to spot and often go undetected.

Fish eagles

Family Accipitridae (part). 10 species in 2 genera

Steller's Sea Eagle has the most powerful bill of any bird of prey

Key features

Heavy bill
Lower legs unfeathered
Rough lower surface to toes
Sexes similar

Fish eagles have long, sharp claws and unfeathered legs. The underside of each toe is covered with rows of sharp spicules, which help it to grip its slippery prey

Fish eagles are amongst the most majestic and attractive of all raptors. These bulky, broad-winged birds are usually brown and white in colour, though they are rather slow developers, with full adult plumage not being attained until their fourth or fifth year of life. The sexes are similar in appearance and difficult to distinguish in the field. Their lower legs are bare as an adaptation to catching fish: the absence of feathers lowers drag through the water as the bird grasps its prey, and prevents waterlogging. They are robust birds with thick feathering that is excellent insulation against the cold. Fish eagles supplement their diet of fish with a range of larger vertebrates, such as foxes, young seals and game birds. They have heavy, sharply hooked bills that enable them to catch and kill prey of such size, as well as deal with carrion.

These birds are always found close to water – near coasts, estuaries, large freshwater lakes and wide rivers. Some species, such as Pallas' Fish Eagle, may occur far inland. The largest, Steller's Sea Eagle, hunts along the bleak coastline of the north Pacific, even amongst the sea ice.

Typical fish eagle behaviour is to sit motionless for long periods on a perch, then to circle over the water in search of prey. These birds are distinctive in flight, with their broad vulture-like wings and slow, heavy wingbeats. They have loud, musical calls that ring out across lakes and still waters. Their large stick nests are usually sited in trees or on cliffs.

White-bellied Sea Eagle
Status: *Local/
declining*
Length: *70-90 cm*
Wingspan: *200 cm*
*Wings of adult grey
above and white
below, with a broad
black border*

*The immature bird
(perched below) is
dark brown with
paler streaks. Buff-
white tail, face and
throat*

Sanford's Sea Eagle
Status: *Threatened*
Length: *80 cm*
Wingspan: *200 cm*
All-brown plumage

The White-bellied (White-breasted) Sea Eagle *Haliaeetus leucogaster* –
one of the smaller sea eagles – is found around the coasts, estuaries,
rivers and swamps of India, South-East Asia, Indonesia and Australia.
It is occasionally seen in populated coastal areas such as Sydney
harbour. While hunting it hovers low over water, dropping down to
catch fish, waterfowl and even sea snakes. This bird often soars slowly
in wide circles with its wings upswept, uttering its distinctive loud,
metallic call.

Sanford's (Solomons) Sea Eagle *Haliaeetus sanfordi* is the only large
eagle in the Solomon Islands. It inhabits inland forests and coastal
areas, but is threatened by deforestation and mining.

African Fish Eagle
Status: *Local*
Length: *74-84 cm*
Wingspan: *215 cm*
Adult has white head and neck and chestnut belly

The immature African Fish Eagle (shown perched below the adult) has black streaking on its breast

Madagascar Fish Eagle
Status: *Endangered/ narrow endemic*
Length: *75 cm*
Wingspan: *185 cm*
Uniform brown plumage, except for white tail

The **African Fish Eagle** *Haliaeetus vocifer* is found on coastal and inland waters in Africa south of the Sahara. Solitary birds or small groups are often seen perched near lakes, or soaring over the water on the lookout for fish. Their prey is either plucked from the surface waters or caught in an Osprey-like plunge dive. In addition to fish, these raptors also take large rodents and waterbirds such as herons, and even flamingos. They are vocal birds with an unmistakable hollow, gull-like ringing call.

The closely related **Madagascar Fish Eagle** *Haliaeetus vociferoides* is restricted to the west coast of the island of Madagascar where there may be as few as 50 pairs.

37

Pallas's Fish Eagle
Status: *Local/
declining*
Length: *80 cm*
Wingspan: *205 cm*
*Adult (above) has
rounded white tail
with dark terminal
band*

*In flight, the adult
bird (right) shows its
dark wings and
rufous belly.
Immature bird
pictured centre*

Pallas' Fish Eagle *Haliaeetus leucoryphus* (also known as Pallas' Sea Eagle and Band-tailed Fish Eagle) is primarily a bird of inland seas, lakes and rivers. Its range extends across central and southern Asia, south to Pakistan, Burma and north India, and to altitudes of up to 4,000 m in Tibet and Ladakh.

These relatively tame birds sometimes build their nests in reedbeds, sand-banks or cliffs, but prefer trees. They take a wide range of prey, including fish, birds, frogs, snakes and carrion and are often seen perched on prominent posts or sand-banks close to water. In some areas, water birds, particularly young of colonial species such as herons and cormorants, form a large part of their diet.

Bald Eagle
Status: *Locally common*
Length: *88 cm (max. 94 cm)*
Wingspan: *210 cm (max. 230 cm)
Massive yellow bill. Adult (left) has distinctive white head and tail*

The immature Bald Eagle (above) has dark plumage with a tawny belly

In flight, the adult bird (above) appears uniform brown, with white head and tail. Immatures (below) have pale markings on wings and tail

The Bald Eagle *Haliaeetus leucocephalus* is the national bird of the USA, and one of the most powerful sea eagles. Its stronghold is Alaska, which is where the largest birds are found. It breeds as far south as Florida, though rarely in the eastern USA. These large raptors often rob other birds, such as Ospreys, of their prey by harrying them until they give up their catch. They congregate in large numbers on salmon spawning rivers to feed on dead and dying fish.

The Bald Eagle's massive nest is added to each season; indeed this species holds the record for the largest tree-nest (nearly 3 m across and 6 m deep). Populations were hit badly by pesticides such as DDT in the 1960s and 1970s, but are now showing signs of recovery.

Fish eagles

<u>White-tailed Eagle</u>
Status: *Vulnerable*
Length: *70-90 cm*
Wingspan: *220 cm*
Adult (left) has white, wedge-shaped tail. Heavy bill

Juvenile (below) is very dark with some pale markings on the tail

The immature bird (in flight, below) is darker than the adult (above). Full adult plumage is achieved in 4-5 years

The **White-tailed (Sea) Eagle** *Haliaeetus albicilla* is the largest of the European eagles. It ranges from Greenland, through Iceland, northern, central and south-eastern Europe, to northern Asia. In Europe it is rather rare except along the coast of Norway and around the Baltic Sea. Attempts to re-introduce the species to Scotland's west coast (centred on the island of Rum) have been successful and a few pairs now breed in that region.

White-tailed Eagles fly low over the water, grabbing fish in their talons: sometimes they launch repeated attacks against seabirds until their prey is too exhausted to escape. They also feed on small mammals and carrion.

Steller's Sea Eagle
Status: *Local/ declining*
Length: *111 cm*
Wingspan: *225 cm (max. 240 cm)*
Huge orange bill. Black plumage with white shoulders (lacking in Korean form), thighs and tail

Juvenile Steller's Sea Eagle (perched left) has uniformly dark plumage except for its mainly white tail

In flight, the juvenile (far left) resembles an adult White-tailed Eagle. The adult (left) has a long, white, wedge-shaped tail and white thighs

Steller's Sea Eagle *Haliaeetus pelagicus* is arguably the world's most powerful eagle, and certainly one of the most beautiful. It breeds only on the Pacific coast of the USSR, along the Bering Sea, Okhotsk Sea and Sakhalin Island, and gathers in the winter off Hokkaido (Shiretoko Peninsula) in Japan, sometimes in large numbers. It is also seen regularly on the Aleutian Islands. The total population is estimated to be around 6,500 birds. This sea eagle has a varied diet of fish, carrion, arctic foxes, young seals and birds including geese.

Like Bald Eagles, Steller's Sea Eagles build huge stick nests in trees or on cliffs, and use these year after year. Again like the Bald Eagle, these birds are attracted in large numbers to feed on salmon when they come up rivers to spawn. They often hunt by watching from a small tree or rock then swooping down to tackle their prey, rather than by circling in the air.

Fish eagles

Greater Fishing Eagle
Status: *Local*
Length: *74 cm*
Wingspan: *160 cm*
*Grey head and neck.
Rounded tail, white
with dark tip*

Lesser Fishing Eagle
Status: *Local*
Length: *55 cm*
Wingspan: *145 cm*
Solid dark brown tail

The **Greater Fishing Eagle** *Ichthyophaga ichthyaetus* (also known as the Grey-headed Fishing Eagle) lives on shores, forest rivers and lakes in India, Sri Lanka, Burma, Malaysia and Indonesia (including Sulawesi). Often perches in waterside trees waiting for fish to rise. This species overlaps with its relative, the Lesser Fishing Eagle *Ichthyophaga humilis* in the eastern part of its range, but the latter species is absent from the Philippines, Java and most of India, except the Himalayan region where it is found at altitudes of up to 1,500 m.

Both species are highly adapted for fishing, having sharp, strongly curved claws and very rough talons with a reversible outer toe, giving an excellent grip on their slippery prey.

Old World vultures

Family Accipitridae (part). 15 species in 6 genera

Key features

Large size
Carrion feeders
Large bill
Bare head/face
Sexes similar

Griffons have long, flexible necks with minimal feathering so they can extract the entrails from a carcase without getting dirty. The bill is sharp enough to rip through tough skin, but narrow enough for precision eating

These broad-winged gliding hunters are restricted to the mountains and plains of Europe, Africa and Asia, and are more closely related to hawks and eagles than to the vultures of the Americas. Most have dark plumage and lack feathers on the head and neck; sexes are similar in appearance. They have a poor sense of smell and rely almost entirely on vision for locating their food: they therefore live in open country where they can easily scan the land below when in flight. In many regions, five or six different vulture species may gather together to feed at a single carcase. In these cases a distinct feeding hierarchy operates, in which the more powerful species chase away the smaller birds by charging them with half-spread wings. At these communal feasts, where vultures are often joined by kites, hawks, jackals, hyenas and lions, a whole antelope may be consumed within an hour.

The Old World vultures, paticularly the griffons, are fierce and competitive feeders, squabbling over the smallest morsel of food. They feed at a phenomenal rate – up to ½ kg of flesh per minute. The engorged birds can scarcely fly away, and may not feed again for up to two weeks.

Old World vultures

Egyptian Vulture
Status: *Locally common*
Length: *60-70 cm*
Wingspan: *155-180 cm*
The adult (in flight, above; perched, above) has creamy white plumage, with black flight feathers

In their first year, Egyptian Vultures are very dark, gradually assuming a lighter plumage as shown (in flight, below). Like the adults, immature birds have bare skin around the face

The Egyptian Vulture *Neophron percnopterus* has a wide range that includes southern Europe (especially Spain, Greece and Turkey), the Middle East, Africa (especially the north-west), south-west and central Asia, and India. In the north of its range it is a summer visitor, migrating to south of the Sahara desert (especially Niger and Sudan) for the winter.

This bird is one of the smallest vultures and often gives way to the larger species when feeding at a carcase. Egyptian vultures are famous for using tools – they sometimes smash open Ostrich eggs with repeated blows from a stone held in the bill. They occasionally raid flamingo and pelican colonies to feed on eggs and young birds.

Lammergeier
Status: *Rare or local*
Length: *100-115 cm*
Wingspan: *266-282 cm*
In flight, the silhouette of both adult (above right) and juvenile (above left) is falcon-like. Reddish or orange below. Wedge-shaped tail. Adult bird has distinctive "moustache"

The Lammergeier *Gypaetus barbatus* is a majestic vulture of mountain country. But with its long tail and relatively narrow, pointed wings, it more closely resembles a gigantic falcon; and unlike most other vultures it takes live food as well as carrion. One of its favoured foods is bone marrow, which it extracts by carrying bones up into the air and dropping them on to jagged rocks below.

Lammergeiers are found from Central Asia and the Himalaya, through the Middle East, to Turkey and Greece (about 40 pairs). They are present on the southern Arabian peninsula, in eastern, southern and north-west Africa (about 100 pairs in Morocco), and also in France and Spain (mainly the Pyrenees, with about 40 pairs).

45

Old World vultures

African White-backed Vulture
Status: *Common*
Length: *90 cm*
Wingspan: *235 cm*
Shown here in flight (below) and on the ground (below right), this raptor has browner plumage than the Indian White-backed vulture. Note the clear white rump

Indian White-backed Vulture
Status: *Common*
Length: *90 cm*
Wingspan: *235 cm*
(Above and below) Less obvious ruff than African species

The Indian (Asian) White-backed Vulture *Gyps bengalensis* is India's commonest vulture. It is often seen near human settlements in India and South-East Asia, where it feeds on refuse and carrion. This colonial bird commonly nests along rivers, but also in towns and villages. Large numbers of these birds gather quickly at animal corpses. Like other griffons, they use their long, flexible necks to reach inside carcases and extract the entrails.

The African White-backed Vulture *Gyps africanus* is the African counterpart of the above species. It is found throughout sub-Saharan Africa, except the Congo basin and the extreme south. This is the species most often seen gathering at kills on the plains and in the National Parks of East Africa. Its range overlaps with that of Rüppell's Griffon (p. 49): it gives way to this larger bird at a kill, and tends to nest in wetter areas.

Griffon Vulture
Status: *Common*
Length: *95-105 cm*
Wingspan: *240-280 cm*
In flight, ragged primaries are visible. Soars with wings slightly upturned

In flight, the immature Griffon (top and third from top) lacks white bands on its coverts

The Griffon's tail is short, dark and square-ended. Its long neck is tucked in when flying

The Griffon Vulture (Eurasian Griffon) *Gyps fulvus* is Europe's commonest large vulture. Its strongholds are in Spain and Turkey, and up to 30 non-breeding birds regularly spend the summer in the Austrian Alps. The range of the species extends eastwards as far as Pakistan and northern India, taking in north-west Africa and the Middle East.

Griffons often circle in small groups before descending to feed together at a carcase. Their large size places them high in the pecking-order, and they give way only to the massive Black and Lappet-faced Vultures (pp. 50 and 51). They nest in colonies of 15-20 pairs on rocky ledges or caves, making nests from sticks and grass.

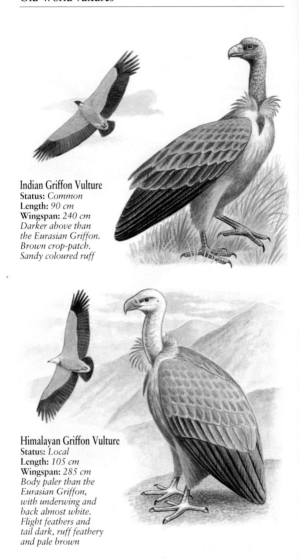

Indian Griffon Vulture
Status: *Common*
Length: *90 cm*
Wingspan: *240 cm*
*Darker above than
the Eurasian Griffon.
Brown crop-patch.
Sandy coloured ruff*

Himalayan Griffon Vulture
Status: *Local*
Length: *105 cm*
Wingspan: *285 cm*
*Body paler than the
Eurasian Griffon,
with underwing and
back almost white.
Flight feathers and
tail dark, ruff feathery
and pale brown*

The Indian Griffon Vulture (Long-billed Griffon) *Gyps indicus* lives on the plains of India and South-East Asia, as well as in the mountains of northern India, including the Himalayan foothills.

The Himalayan Griffon Vulture *Gyps himalayensis* is the largest of all the griffons. It is very similar to the Eurasian Griffon (p. 47) and replaces that species at high altitude in the Himalaya and mountains of central Asia. In some places (such as Kashmir) both species may occur together. Himalayan griffons soar at high altitudes, and often follow each other to likely food sources.

Rüppell's Griffon Vulture
Status: *Common*
Length: *85-95 cm*
Wingspan: *220-250 cm*
*Distinctive white bar
and two rows of
white spots on
underside of wings*

Rüppell's Griffon Vulture *Gyps ruepellii* is another very close relative of the Eurasian Griffon, replacing it in north-east, east and central Africa, where it inhabits mountains, dry plains and deserts. It is a sociable vulture which flocks to carrion and often soars in groups, sometimes reaching great heights. Indeed, this species holds the record for the highest observed avian flight – 11,274 m.

Cape Griffon
Status: *Rare/declining*
Length: *90 cm*
Wingspan: *250 cm*
*Almost white body,
pale buff ruff. Flight
feathers and tail
sooty-brown*

The Cape Griffon (Cape Vulture) *Gyps coprotheres* is also very closely related to Eurasian Griffon, but it is slightly smaller. The species is restricted to the hills and dry plains of southern Africa where it has become rare in recent decades. Its total population now stands at less than 10,000.

Its pale colour and markings are similar to those of the larger Himalayan Griffon. This species has suffered from a shortage of carcases on which to feed, as game animals have decreased in many areas, and since many farmers now routinely bury dead livestock.

European Black Vulture
Status: *Local/ declining*
Length: *100-110 cm*
Wingspan: *250-295 cm*
All-dark plumage and deep bill. Pale feet visible even at long range. Wings are long and broad with parallel edges. Tail often seems wedge-shaped

Juvenile (bottom) is very dark, appearing black at a distance. The bill (cere) and neck become colourful with age

The **European Black Vulture** *Aegypius monachus*, at a weight of up to 12 kg, is the largest and heaviest of the Old World Vultures, and the third largest bird of prey in the world, after the American Condors. It is a solitary bird found in mountainous country with a scattered distribution in Europe (mainly Spain and Turkey), Caucasus and southern and central Asia, east to China and Taiwan. It wanders as far south as Sudan outside the breeding season. There are only about 400 pairs in southern Europe, including several pairs in Mallorca, where they are seriously threatened. Black Vultures usually build their nests in trees, especially in pines, oaks or junipers growing on rocky slopes. They are dominant over other species at a carcase.

Lappet-faced Vulture
Status: *Rare (Israel and Morocco); uncommon (rest of Africa)*
Length: *95-105 cm*
Wingspan: *255-290 cm*
White thighs, bright pink skin on face, very heavy bill. Huge wingspan

Wings and tail appear dark in flight. White feathers on thighs and along wing coverts.

The **Lappet-faced Vulture** (**Nubian Vulture**) *Aegypius tracheliotus* is the largest vulture found in Africa, where it takes prime position at kills. This voracious feeder can rip open the skin of recently-killed mammals by swiping sideways with its large, sharp bill. It also steals food from other vultures and has even been recorded killing young birds, such as flamingos, for itself. It is most likely to be seen in the National Parks of Kenya, or in Chad, where it is local. It usually nests in isolated pairs, building a large stick nest in the crown of a tall tree.

Lappet-faced Vultures sometimes follow flocks of Griffons or Hooded Vultures in order to find their prey. These smaller species move aside to let the huge Lappet-faced Vultures feed at leisure.

51

Red-headed Vulture
Status: *Common*
Length: *76 cm*
Wingspan: *200 cm*
Black plumage, scarlet head, neck and legs. Whitish band on underside of wings in flight. Wings held in shallow V

White-headed Vulture
Status: *Local*
Length: *76 cm*
Wingspan: *200 cm*
White head, white belly, red and blue bill. Adult has white secondaries

The **Red-headed Vulture** *Aegypius calvus,* also known as the Indian Black Vulture, Pondicherry Vulture or King Vulture, is a black, turkey-like bird found in the Indian subcontinent (to 2,000 m in Himalaya), Burma, Thailand, Malaya and Vietnam. It is, however, absent from Sri Lanka. Despite its large size it is timid and low in the pecking-order at a carcase.

The White-headed Vulture *Aegypius occipitalis* is a bird of Africa, south of the Sahara. It sometimes kills its own prey, including large lizards and often chooses a Baobab or *Acacia* tree in which to build its stick nest. It is most frequently found in the National Parks of Kenya and Tanzania.

Hooded Vulture
Status: *Common*
Length: *62-72 cm*
Wingspan: *170 cm*
Small, dark brown bird with short, rounded tail. Thin bill, pink face, white crop-patch. In flight, the tail is shorter than the Egyptian Vulture's

The **Hooded Vulture** *Necrosyrtes monachus* is a small bird, similar in build to the Egyptian Vulture (p.44), whose range it shares in Africa south of the Sahara. In addition to carrion, Hooded Vultures eat a wide range of food, including fish and crustaceans at the shore, lizards, and scraps of rubbish. Their small size relegates them to near the bottom of the pecking-order at a carcase. Nesting is either solitary or in small colonies, in trees or on cliffs. The Hooded Vulture is more sociable than the Egyptian Vulture and is often seen feeding or flying in small groups. It is also more common than the latter species throughout most of its range. At a distance it resembles an immature Egyptian Vulture.

Palm-nut Vulture
Status: *Uncommon*
Length: *56-62 cm*
Wingspan: *150 cm*
*Striking black and
white plumage. Black
secondaries stand out
in flight, as does
white tip of tail*

The **Palm-nut Vulture** *Gypohierax angolensis* is the most unusual of
all the Old World Vultures, not least because it is mainly vegetarian. In
build it more like a fish-eagle than a vulture and indeed was formerly
known as the Vulturine Fish Eagle. Its unique diet comprises the flesh
of Oil Palm nuts and the fruits of *Raffia* as well as fish, crabs, crayfish,
molluscs, and carrion. This vulture's preferred habitats are mangroves,
wooded savanna and tropical forest, in Africa south of the Sahara. It is
common on Pemba Island, Tanzania.

The Palm-nut Vulture is similar in size and overall colouration to
the Egyptian Vulture, though it has a different flight shape, with
broad, rounded wings and a square tail.

Snake eagles

Family Accipitridae (part). 15 species in 5 genera

The true snake eagles, like this Short-toed Eagle, have flat faces and forward-facing eyes. Short, tight facial feathers protect them from snake bites

Key features

Large size
Short, powerful toes
Sexes similar

Serpent eagles, like this Crested Serpent Eagle, have erectile crests that can be fanned out to form a halo. The crest may help the bird to locate sounds, or serve a function in courtship displays

Key features

Grey or brown plumage
Many have crest

This group comprises six true snake eagles, eight serpent eagles and the the bulky, atypical African Bateleur. All are large but graceful birds, and feed mostly on snakes and other reptiles. They are usually grey or brown in plumage, and the sexes are difficult to distinguish in the field.

The true snake eagles are elegant buzzard-sized raptors, with flat, harrier-like faces and keen eyesight. They typically soar and hover over scrub and rocky hillsides where snakes and lizards are likely to be sunning themselves. Having grasped a snake in their powerful claws, they kill it with a bite to the head or neck. Of the true snake eagles, only the Short-toed Eagle is found outside Africa. They are vocal birds, making loud calls while circling high overhead.

Of the serpent eagles, six are members of the genus *Spilornis*, the most common and widespread being the Crested Serpent Eagle. This species is highly variable in both size and plumage, and may easily be mistaken for other members of the genus. The *Spilornis* serpent eagles are all Indian or South-East Asian birds. They have shorter wings than the true snake eagles, and a distinctive fan-shaped erectile crest at the back of the head. The two remaining serpent eagles (Congo and Madagascar) are not closely related, either to each other, or to other members of the group. They are *Accipiter*-like in build, and inhabit dense forest.

55

Bateleur

When in the air, the Bateleur's feet extend beyond its short tail. Pictured here in flight: adult female (above), immature bird (below)

Bateleur
Status: *Common*
Length: *80-85 cm*
Wingspan: *170-180 cm*
The immature bird (right) has mainly brown plumage

The adult Bateleur (male above, female below right) has black underparts that contrast with its white wings, a large facial ruff and bright red bare skin on its face

The Bateleur (Eagle) *Terathopius ecaudatus* inhabits savanna, bush and semi-desert in mainland sub-Saharan Africa. It spends much of its time soaring and has a highly distinctive rocking flight motion from which it derives its name ("bateleur" is French for "tightrope walker"). The rocking motion allows this eagle to steer in the absence of a longer tail. Bateleurs feed mainly on small mammals, birds, and reptiles. They also eat carrion and often steal food from other raptors, such as vultures. Bateleurs put on impressive flight displays in the breeding season. The male flies high above the female over their territory and goes into a steep dive. The female then rolls over in mid-air to grapple talons as her mate approaches.

56

Short-toed Eagle
Status: *Local (Europe)*
Length: *62-67 cm*
Wingspan: *185-195 cm*
Frequently hovers. Head protrudes in flight

Almost pure white below, dark above. Larger than buzzard. Scaly legs, feathered at the base, and short, tight feathering on head and neck help protect the bird from snakebites

The Short-toed Eagle *Circaetus gallicus* is distributed from India and south-west Asia, with an outpost in the Lesser Sundas (Bali to Timor), through the Middle East and north-west Africa to southern and eastern Europe, where its strongholds are Spain, southern France and Turkey. It is the only snake eagle resident in Europe.

Short-toed Eagles hunt mainly in dry, stony areas with a plentiful supply of snakes, but will also scour adjacent wetlands for grass snakes. They soar and hover over such terrain, dropping down on to snakes, which they kill by crushing in their short, powerful toes. They can occasionally be seen returning to their nests with prey hanging down from their bills.

Brown Snake Eagle
Status: *Locally common*
Length: *68 cm*
Wingspan: *190 cm*
Entirely dark brown. Three narrow pale bars in tail

Black-chested Snake Eagle
Status: *Local*
Length: *65 cm*
Wingspan: *185 cm*
Black chest, pure white belly and undersides of wings. Immature bird brown above, pale rufous below

Beaudouin's Snake Eagle
Status: *Rare*
Length: *65 cm*
Wingspan: *185 cm*
Similar to Black-chested Snake Eagle, but note streaked throat

The Brown Snake Eagle *Circaetus cinereus* occurs in dry savannas in most African countries south of Sahara, though it is absent from the Congo basin. In East Africa, where it is rather local, this bird is often seen in Baobab trees.

The Black-chested Snake Eagle *Circaetus pectoralis* is a native of eastern and southern Africa. In east Africa, it occurs most frequently in Kenya's Rift Valley, northern Kenya and Uganda.

The distribution of Beaudouin's Snake Eagle *Circaetus beaudouini* follows the southern edge of the Sahara, from Senegal to Sudan. It is also known from the Mara Reserve in Kenya. The latter two species are known to interbreed with the Short-toed Eagle (p. 57).

Banded Snake Eagle
Status: *Local*
Length: *61 cm*
Wingspan: *180 cm*
*Black tail has broad
white band*

**Southern Banded
Snake Eagle**
Status: *Local*
Length: *63 cm*
Wingspan: *182 cm*
Barred tail

The (Smaller) Banded Snake Eagle *Circaetus cinerascens* is a bird of tropical Africa. In its favoured habitats – swamp country and riverside forest – it feeds on snakes, lizards and frogs.

Like the above species, the Southern Banded Snake Eagle *Circaetus fasciolatus* is small in build compared to the other members of its genus. The ranges of the two birds overlap from southern Somalia to Mozambique, but the Southern Banded Snake Eagle, which is also a forest bird, replaces the Banded Snake Eagle in south-east Africa.

Neither of these snake eagles are easily observed. They are both rather shy and secretive, and breed and hunt in thick inaccessible tropical forest.

Crested Serpent Eagle
Status: *Common*
Length: *50-71 cm*
Wingspan: *145 cm*
Ruff-like dark crest.
Black bands on
wings. Wags tail on
landing

Philippine Serpent Eagle
Status: *Common*
Length: *50 cm*
Wingspan: *120 cm*
Spotted white
underparts

Sulawesi Serpent Eagle
Status: *Local/narrow*
endemic
Length: *48 cm*
Wingspan: *115 cm*
Black head and neck,
amber chest

The Crested Serpent Eagle *Spilornis cheela* is the most widespread member of its genus. Found in India, southern China, Taiwan, South-East Asia, Malaysia, and Indonesia east to Borneo, it varies considerably in size and plumage, and is difficult to observe since it usually keeps to the cover of forests. From its perch, it scours the ground for its prey of small rodents, reptiles, amphibians and birds.

The Philippine Serpent Eagle *Spilornis holospilus* lives in forest clearings and open woodland in the Philippines.

The Sulawesi Serpent Eagle *Spilornis rufipectus* (of Sulawesi and north-west Borneo) is a small, dark forest bird which preys on snakes, lizards and small rodents.

Kinabalu Serpent Eagle
Status: *Rare/narrow endemic*
Length: *50 cm*
Wingspan: *120 cm*
Feeds mainly on snakes, like other members of the genus

Andaman Serpent Eagle
Status: *Rare/narrow endemic*
Length: *56 cm*
Wingspan: *134 cm*
Plumage dark brown, sometimes with a rufous tinge. Heavily spotted below

Nicobar Serpent Eagle
Status: *Rare/narrow endemic*
Length: *45 cm (38 cm in Southern form)*
Wingspan: *106 cm*
Pale cinnamon below

The Kinabalu Serpent Eagle *Spilornis kinabaluensis* is known only from Sabah and Sarawak, Malaysia. Although not well studied, its small population is thought to be at risk through habitat loss.

The Andaman Serpent Eagle (Dark Serpent Eagle) *Spilornis elgini* is endemic to the Andaman Islands in the Bay of Bengal, where it inhabits forest clearings.

The Nicobar Serpent Eagle *Spilornis minimus*, which is restricted to the Nicobar Islands (south of the Andamans), is the world's smallest eagle. A diminutive form of this bird lives on Great Nicobar Island: it is recognized by some as a separate species – the Southern Nicobar Serpent Eagle (*Spilornis klossi*).

Congo Serpent Eagle
Status: *Local*
Length: *56 cm*
Wingspan: *90 cm*
*Rufous brown above,
white below. Sparsely
spotted. Dark
moustache, black
stripe on throat*

Madagascar Serpent Eagle
Status: *Endangered/
narrow endemic*
Length: *56 cm*
Wingspan: *90 cm*
*Grey plumage with
short crest*

The Congo Serpent Eagle *Dryotriorchis spectabilis* is the sole representative of its genus. It lives in the dense primary forest of west and central Africa – a habitat to which it is well adapted. Its short wings and long tail enable it to manoeuvre between the trees as it seeks out its prey of reptiles, amphibians and small mammals, and its large eyes help it see more clearly in the gloomy forest interior.

The Madagascar Serpent Eagle *Eutriorchis astur* is an unusual species, with short wings, long tail, and bristles at the base of its upper mandible. Accordingly it is classified in its own genus. This rare bird has hardly ever been seen let alone studied, and may now be nearing extinction as its tropical forest habitat is cleared.

Harrier hawks and Crane Hawk

Family Accipitridae (part). 3 species in 2 genera

An African Harrier Hawk is shown here probing a crevice in a tree trunk in search of food

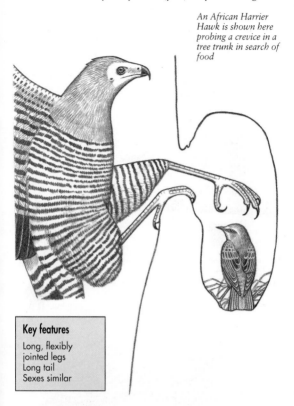

Key features

Long, flexibly jointed legs
Long tail
Sexes similar

These medium-sized, long-tailed hawks are mostly grey in colour. The sexes are similar in appearance. All have double-jointed legs, with which they probe cavities in trees for their prey, which consists mostly of nestlings and insects. They will also take bats and small mammals, such as squirrels.

The two harrier hawks are closely related and are both African residents. Distinctive plumage and behaviour sets them apart from other birds of prey: their vulture-like faces have large areas of tough orange or yellow skin, which may offer some protection against insect bites and the defensive lunges of nesting birds; their long legs and slow-flapping flight give them a rather ungainly appearance. Harrier hawks inhabit forest and savanna and build large nests from sticks and leaves, in which they lay one or two eggs per year. The young hatch after about 35 days.

The Crane Hawk is the South American equivalent of the harrier hawks. It too uses its double-jointed legs to search inside crevices for birds, eggs and invertebrates, including the larvae of bees. Crane Hawks also eat snakes, including poisonous coral snakes. They are attracted to grass fires, where they pounce on reptiles and large insects fleeing the heat and flames. These birds lack the bare facial skin of the harrier hawks.

Harrier hawks

African Hawk Harrier
Status: *Locally common*
Length: *64 cm*
Wingspan: *140 cm*
Tail long, wide and black, with broad white band. Black and white bars on belly. Loose crest

Madagascar Harrier Hawk
Status: *Local*
Length: *64 cm*
Wingspan: *140 cm*

Silver-grey head. Lacks black spots above

The African Harrier Hawk *(Gymnogene) Polyboroides typus* is found in a wide range of habitats, including woodland and savanna, in Africa south of the Sahara. Its different hunting strategies reflect its varied diet. This bird searches on the ground for invertebrates, and also uses its double jointed legs to probe crevices in trees for insects, small mammals, birds and eggs. It also includes Oil Palm fruit in its diet.

The Madagascar Harrier Hawk *Polyboroides radiatus* is restricted to Madagascar where it lives in wooded areas up to about 1,500 m. In the north-east of the island it frequently visits banana plantations, seraching for lizards to supplement its diet of locusts and amphibians.

The Mexican race of Crane Hawk is very dark. Others are mostly pale grey and barred below. All races have a banded black and white tail

Crane Hawk
Status: *Locally common*
Length: *45 cm*
Wingspan: *98 cm*
Broad, rounded wings and long, rounded tail

The Crane Hawk *Geranospiza caerulescens* is a less powerful bird than the harrier hawks (p. 64), though this South American species occupies a similar ecological niche to its African relatives. Like the harrier hawks, it has long, flexibly jointed legs with which it probes cracks and crevices in tree trunks in its search for food – chiefly insect larvae, eggs and young birds. Again, like the harrier hawks, it often seeks out its prey in a rather slow and deliberate way.

The Crane Hawk is most commonly seen in wet woodland and swampy habitats from Mexico to Argentina, but it also hunts lizards over dry country, sailing low over the ground in the manner of a harrier.

Several discrete regional races are recognized: the basic plumage pattern is consistent and the birds differ mainly in colour. In parts of Mexico, a slate-grey form predominates, whilst both dark and pale forms occur south of the Amazon.

Harriers

Family Accipitridae (part). 10 species in 1 genus

The deep V-shaped silhouette of the Hen Harrier is typical of the group

The Hen Harrier's flat face, with its disc-like feathering, recalls an owl

Key features

Long wings
Long tail
Facial ruff
Buoyant, gliding flight

Harriers are slender, medium-sized hawks with long wings, tails and legs. They have rather flat faces with the eyes directed forwards to ensure good binocular vision. The sexes differ in plumage: males are usually grey and white, or black and white; females are brown.

Harriers hunt by gliding low over open country, scanning the ground below for birds or small mammals. In flight they appear buoyant and often hold their wings in a V. Nearly all nest on the ground amongst low bushes, grasses or reedbeds. Between three and eight eggs are laid each season, hatching after about 30 days.

Like many other hawks, harriers indulge in elaborate courtship displays early in the breeding season. The male Marsh Harrier, for example, soars to a great height (often out of sight) above the breeding territory, and then descends to the ground in a spectacular sequence of rolls, tumbles and free-fall flight. The female sometimes joins in these displays, and the pair indulge in mock battles, grappling talons and tumbling through the air together. Later in the season the male can be seen transferring food to the female in mid-air by dropping it into her talons as she flies upside-down below him.

Marsh Harrier

Status: *Locally common*
Length: *48-56 cm*
Wingspan: *115-130 cm*
Adult female (below) appears almost black at a distance

In flight, the adult male (above) shows black wingtips, and grey head and breast

Typical adult female (below) has cream-coloured head, throat and leading edge of upper wing, though these markings do vary

Typical adult male (above) is russet brown with grey areas on wings and tail

The Marsh Harrier *Circus aeruginosus* is distributed from Europe and North Africa through the Middle East and much of north and central Asia, into the southern hemisphere, notably Madagascar, Australia (where it is known as the Swamp Harrier) and New Zealand. In Europe it is increasing in the north, but decreasing in most of the south and east. The Marsh Harrier is well-named, preferring thick swampy habitats, especially those with extensive reedbeds, over which it hunts by gliding low with long wings held in a V. A common flight pattern consists of between five and ten wingbeats, interspersed with periods of gliding. It feeds on a wide range of prey, including water birds, small mammals, fish, amphibians and invertebrates.

African Marsh Harrier
Status: *Local*
Length: *46-51 cm*
Wingspan: *120 cm*
Dark, rufous-brown plumage. Smaller than the Marsh Harrier with no white rump. Tail and flight feathers are barred black

Black Harrier
Status: *Uncommon/ narrow endemic*
Length: *50 cm*
Wingspan: *120 cm*
Black plumage with white rump and barred tail. Flight feathers white, tipped black

The **African Marsh Harrier** *Circus ranivorus* inhabits marshes, reedbeds and adjacent farmlands from Kenya and Uganda south to the Cape region. In Kenya and southern Tanzania it is found in high moorland and swamps, open plains and farmland, and sometimes also at lake margins.

The Black Harrier *Circus maurus* is a rather rare species with a limited distribution. It is found mainly in dry country in southern Africa, and in the mountains of the Cape and Natal. It hunts, often alone, in typical harrier fashion, flying low over both wet and dry country on the lookout for small mammals, amphibians, birds and large insects.

Hen Harrier

Status: *Common/local*
Length: *44-52 cm*
Wingspan: *100-120 cm*
Male (above and right) has gull-like plumage, but note the white rump

The female Hen Harrier (below and left) is brown with a banded tail. Also has white rump. Similar to Montagu's Harrier, but heavier in build. The young of both sexes resemble the adult female

The Hen Harrier *Circus cyaneus* is found in North America and northern Asia, as well as in its European strongholds of France, Sweden, Finland, Spain and the British Isles. It is the only harrier resident in North America, where it is also known as the Northern Harrier or Marsh Hawk. In this part of its range it breeds from mid-latitudes up into the boreal forests of Canada and Alaska.

Hen Harriers inhabit moorland, marshes, dunes and grassland and feed on small rodents, birds, amphibians, reptiles and some insects. They are typically seen gliding low over open country watching and listening for any sign of prey on the ground below. They build their nests on the ground, hidden amongst tall vegetation.

Harriers

Adult male Montagu's Harrier (far left) has a grey rump, black wing-bars and brown streaks on its belly and thighs. The female (left) has less white on the rump. The immmature bird (below) is rufous below

Montagu's Harrier
Status: *Local*
Length: *43-47 cm*
Wingspan: *110 cm*
More slender in build than the Hen Harrier

The adult male Pallid Harrier (below) has distinctive black markings on its wing-tips

Pallid Harrier
Status: *Local*
Length: *40-48 cm*
Wingspan: *110 cm*
The male bird (pictured right) has a grey rump and whitish head and upperparts

Montagu's Harrier *Circus pygargus* is found on the plains of central and south-west Asia, and has a scattered distribution in Europe where its main centres of population are France (especially Alsace) and Spain. A handful of pairs nest in England. Its prefers plains, moorland and lake and marsh habitats, but also breeds in cereal fields and grassland. These birds migrate in large numbers over Gibraltar to spend the winter in Africa.

The Pallid *Harrier Circus macrourus* is a bird of the steppes of central Asia, west to the Black Sea area. A few pairs breed in Romania and Bulgaria. Pallid Harriers winter mainly in India and eastern Africa, but migrants are often seen in Europe and the Middle East.

Cinereous Harrier
Status: *Local*
Length: *45 cm*
Wingspan: *105 cm*
Similar to the Hen Harrier (p.69), but slightly smaller. The male (left and above left) is barred below; the female (above right) is barred below in amber and white

Long-winged Harrier
Status: *Local*
Length: *55 cm*
Wingspan: *135 cm*
Male is chocolate black above with white rump. Pale below (dark phase is dark below). Black head and neck with white eyebrow. Female is browner and more heavily spotted below

The Cinereous Harrier *Circus cinereus* lives in grassland and marshes in South America, from Colombia south to Tierra del Fuego. It is found at a range of altitudes from the lowlands right up to 4,000 m. This species is like a smaller version of the Hen Harrier (p. 69), and occupies a similar ecological niche in southern South America.

The Long-winged Harrier *Circus buffoni* is most common in Colombia, the Guianas and Trinidad, but also occurs in Argentina, eastern Bolivia and Chile. It lives on the pampas – or marshland – and feeds on small birds, mammals and amphibians, caught in typical harrier fashion. Like many other harriers, this bird nests on the ground in amongst marsh vegetation.

71

Harriers

Spotted Harrier
Status: *Common (inland and northern Australia)*
Length: *50-61 cm*
Wingspan: *135 cm*
Blue-grey above with white spots. Narrow bands on tail. Chestnut face and underparts

The female Pied Harrier (below) resembles the female Pallid Harrier but with heavier streaking on the underparts

Pied Harrier
Status: *Local*
Length: *46-51 cm*
Wingspan: *115 cm*
The male bird, pictured above and in flight below, has unmistakable black, white and grey plumage

The Spotted Harrier *Circus assimilis* (also known as the Allied Harrier, Smoke Hawk or Spotted Swamp Hawk) is perhaps the most beautiful of all the harriers. It prefers open plains and grassy scrubland and is found throughout most of Australia, Sulawesi and the Lesser Sunda Islands. It feeds on small mammals, birds, reptiles and insects.

The Pied Harrier *Circus melanoleucos* occupies open steppe and wetland habitats in east Siberia, Mongolia, North Korea and Burma. It spends the winter in India, Burma and Sri Lanka, and can often be seen feeding over rice paddies. This small and rather delicate bird includes many insects in its diet. It builds its nest amongst grasses, rushes and other low vegetation, laying up to five eggs per season.

Sparrowhawks and goshawks

Family Accipitridae (part). 52 species in 2 genera

Broad wings and a long tail are typical of this group. Wing tips are less pointed than in the falcons

Goshawks have compact but powerful bills, hooked at the tip, but lacking the notch of the falcons

The legs of Accipiter *hawks are long. The toes have distinct bumps beneath*

The sparrowhawks and goshawks are designed for stealth and speed in wooded areas. They typically have short, rounded wings and long tails, a combination which makes for great mobility in a restricted space. They hunt by surprise, ambushing their prey (usually other birds) in flight. On the whole, these birds are grey or brown above, and barred below, though the sexes differ in appearance, with females generally larger than males. This size difference enables the sexes to concentrate upon different prey, thereby increasing feeding efficiency.

The largest species (often called goshawks) are similar in size to the smaller buzzards and buzzard-like hawks. The smaller species tend to be known as sparrowhawks. Of the members of the group, 49 are very similar in body plan and belong to the single genus *Accipiter*. The group also contains the two species of chanting goshawks and the Gabar Goshawk, which all belong to the genus *Melierax*.

The majority of species are found in the tropics, particularly South-East Asia and Indonesia. Of those present in northern temperate regions, the Northern Goshawk, Eurasian Sparrowhawk and Sharp-shinned Hawk are by far the most common and widespread.

Sparrowhawks and goshawks usually build compact nests in trees and lay between two and five eggs per season, which hatch after about 28 to 50 days, depending on the species.

Chanting goshawks

Wings rather rounded in flight. Pale secondaries contrast with dark primaries. Flight action similar to Accipiter hawks

Dark Chanting Goshawk
Status: *Local*
Length: *38-48 cm*
Wingspan: *95-110 cm*
Long legs and grey-barred rump. Cere orange-red

Pale Chanting Goshawk
Status: *Locally common*
Length: *40-50 cm*
Wingspan: *110-125 cm*

Lighter plumage than above species, with clear white rump. Legs bright orange-red, cere yellow

Both species circle high over breeding territory at the start of the season

The Dark Chanting Goshawk *Melierax metabates* lives in much of sub-Saharan Africa and south-west Arabia with an isolated population in central Morocco. It is replaced by the Pale Chanting Goshawk *Melierax canorus* in eastern and southern Africa. The latter species is particularly common in eastern and northern Kenya, where the ranges of the two birds overlap in places.

Chanting goshawks inhabit dry bushland and semi-deserts. From their perches on posts or in trees, they sit and wait for their prey - mainly lizards, but also birds, mammals and large insects. Their name comes from the clear piping call made by the male birds at the start of the breeding season.

Gabar Goshawk
Status: *Common*
Length: *31-38 cm*
Wingspan: *85 cm*
Smaller than Chanting Goshawk. White-banded tail. The adult male bird (left) resembles female Little Sparrowhawk (p. 92)

The female Gabar Goshawk (right) is noticeably larger than the male. This may enable the sexes to specialize on different prey

A black form of the Gabar Goshawk (left) occurs, especially in dense forested country. Similar to the Ovampo Sparrowhawk (p. 91), but with white patches on flight feathers

The Gabar Goshawk *Melierax gabar* is found in wooded country and savanna throughout sub-Saharan Africa. It is intermediate in looks and behaviour between the chanting goshawks and the true *Accipiter* hawks. It takes much less of its food on the ground than the *Accipiters:* its feeding strategy is similar to that of the sparrowhawk, in that it catches small birds (especially Weaver Finches) in flight.

The Gabar Goshawk is much less vocal than the chanting goshawks, and has a more sparrowhawk-like chittering alarm note. In the breeding season these birds are very active, chasing each other in and out of the trees. They build stick nests high up in tall trees, sometimes incorporating spiders' webs for camouflage.

Goshawks and relatives

Goshawk
Status: *Local*
Length: *48-65 cm*
Wingspan: *115-165 cm*

Note protruding, almost triangular head in flight. Body powerful with broad chest

Adult female (above) is significantly larger than male (above right)

Juvenile has bold streaks below and blotched markings above. Full adult plumage at about 2 years

The (**Northern**) **Goshawk** *Accipiter gentilis* is a large, buzzard-sized forest hunter, found throughout the northern hemisphere. It breeds only in large tracts of woodland (particularly coniferous forests), so unsurprisingly its European strongholds are in Sweden and Finland, but the small British population is slowly increasing. In North America it is found mostly in northern and mountain forests.

Goshawks feed mainly upon medium-sized birds and mammals such as jays, crows, pigeons, rabbits and squirrels, which they kill in surprise attacks that incorporate rapid surges of speed. The Goshawk's name comes from the Anglo-Saxon word for "goose-hawk".

Goshawks are often persecuted because they kill game birds, though mostly weak or sick birds are taken.

Red Goshawk
Status: *Rare/declining*
Length: *50-60 cm*
Wingspan: *120 cm*
Distinctive underwing pattern

Rusty red colour. Similar in size to Northern Goshawk, but has slightly longer wings

Doria's Goshawk
Status: *Local/narrow endemic*
Length: *50 cm*
Wingspan: *90 cm*
Short wings and extremely long tail. Dark brown above, pale below. Short crest

The **Red Goshawk** *Accipiter radiatus* (also known as the Red Buzzard and Rufous-bellied Buzzard) is a powerful hunter, capable of killing birds as large as cockatoos. This rarely-observed species is found in northern and eastern Australia where it favours wooded hilly country and waterways edged with trees. Its alternative name of Red Buzzard comes from its habit of soaring, buzzard-like, over open country when searching for likely prey. Red Goshawks usually nest high in the branches of tall trees, often in abandoned crows' nests.

Doria's Goshawk *Accipiter doriae* of New Guinea lives in forests from sea level to about 1,500 m. It is a shy species and has been little studied. Similar to juvenile Bürger's Sparrowhawk (p. 84), which also occurs in New Guinea.

African Goshawk
Status: *Common/local*
Length: *36-43 cm*
Wingspan: *80 cm*
*Slate grey above,
barred brown below
with rufous wash.
Female paler and
much larger than
male*

Great Sparrowhawk
Status: *Local*
Length: *46-56 cm*
Wingspan: *120 cm*
*Slate-black above,
white below with
black patch above
thighs. Long tail*

The African Goshawk *Accipiter tachiro* is a species of woodland and forest in Africa south of the Sahara desert. While common in certain areas - such as the highland forests of Kenya - this bird is secretive in its habits and therefore seldom seen. This species uses the typical bird-hawk hunting method of hot pursuit and ambush, making good use of tree-cover to surprise its prey.

The Great (or Black) Sparrowhawk *Accipiter melanoleucus* (sometimes known as the Black and White Goshawk) is also a bird of African upland forests, though it is more common in the west than in eastern and southern Africa. In build it resembles the Northern Goshawk (p. 76).

Australian Goshawk
Status: *Common*
Length: *40-55 cm*
Wingspan: *To 100 cm*
The male bird (left and in flight) is markedly smaller than the female (below)

Collared Sparrowhawk
Status: *Common*
Length: *30-40 cm*
Wingspan: *To 76 cm*
Slightly forked tail visible when perched. Distinct rufous collar. The male bird is pictured right, the female bottom left

The **Australian Goshawk** (**Brown Goshawk**) *Accipiter fasciatus* is common in woodland, shelter-belts and farmland throughout Australia and Tasmania, and is occasionally seen in parks and gardens. It also occurs in New Guinea and Indonesia, Christmas Island (Indian Ocean), The Lesser Sunda Islands, The New Hebrides, New Caledonia and Fiji. Introduced rabbits now form an important part of the diet of the Australian Goshawk, although the range of prey taken is quite wide, and includes birds and reptiles.

The (Australian) **Collared Sparrowhawk** *Accipiter cirrocephalus* lives in rainforest, scrub and timbered gorges throughout Australia, Tasmania and New Guinea.

Variable Goshawk
Status: *Locally common*
Length: *40-50 cm*
Wingspan: *100 cm*
Whites phase (above and left) bears a striking resemblance to the Sulphur-crested Cockatoo

Grey phase (right) is pale grey above, and usually has faint barring on the underside

The vinous-chested form (below and in flight) has a chestnut underside

The Variable Goshawk *Accipiter novaehollandiae* is primarily a species of rainforests and forested waterways. It has a number of distinct colour phases, each of which is found in a specific part of the bird's range or in a particular type of habitat.

In Australia the grey phase dominates in coastal rainforest, while the white phase is predominant in the Kimberleys (Western Australia) and in Tasmania. The species also occurs in New Guinea, Maluku (the Moluccas) and in the Solomon Islands, where the darkest forms are found. The Solomon Islands – specifically New Georgia and Bougainville – are also home to the vinous-chested form of the Variable Goshawk.

Asian Crested Goshawk
Status: *Local*
Length: *30-40 cm*
Wingspan: *65 cm*
Brown above, white below. White throat divided by black streak. Short crest and short, rounded wings. Closely resembles Jerdon's Baza (p. 17)

Sulawesi Crested Goshawk
Status: *Unknown*
Length: *30 cm*
Wingspan: *75 cm*
Slate-blue head. Underparts white, breast heavily streaked brown

The **Asian Crested Goshawk** *Accipiter trivirgatus* is found in the tropical forests of southern India and Sri Lanka, and in an area stretching from the eastern Himalayan foothills, through Burma and South-East Asia to Taiwan, the Philippines and Indonesia. It varies considerably in size across its range, the largest individuals occuring in northern India, the smallest in the Philippines. Its resemblance to Jerdon's Baza probably evolved through natural selection, though the advantage to either species is as yet unclear.

The **Sulawesi Crested Goshawk** *Accipiter griseiceps* is a little-known species from the forests and mangroves of Sulawesi. It takes a variety of prey, including small birds, small mammals, lizards and insects.

Goshawks and relatives

Fiji Goshawk
Status: *Common/
narrow endemic*
Length: *28-38 cm*
Wingspan: *70 cm
Pinkish colour on
nape and underparts.
Barring absent from
wings and tail*

Grey-headed Goshawk
Status: *Locally
common/narrow
endemic*
Length: *30-38 cm*
Wingspan: *70 cm
Grey above, white
below. Similar in
appearance to the
New Britain Grey-
headed Goshawk (p.
83) but somewhat
smaller*

The **Fiji Goshawk** *Accipiter rufitorques* is endemic to the islands of the Fiji archipelago, where it is the only *Accipiter* present. Its prey includes small birds, reptiles and large insects. These birds have been observed in parks and gardens as well as forests.

The (New Guinea) **Grey-headed Goshawk** *Accipiter poliocephalus* is restricted to New Guinea and certain nearby islands. It lives in forests and along their margins, and is reported to feed on small reptiles and large insects.

Both the above species and the Grey Frog Hawk lack the obvious barring pattern on their undersides that characterizes other members of the genus *Accipiter*.

New Britain Grey-headed Goshawk
Status: *Uncommon/narrow endemic*
Length: *38-43 cm*
Wingspan: *85 cm*
Grey above, white below. Breast faintly barred. Closely resembles New Guinea Grey-headed Goshawk (p. 82), but somewhat larger

Grey Frog Hawk
Status: *Locally common*
Length: *26-35 cm*
Wingspan: *65 cm*
Slate-grey above, white below (unbarred). Relatively long wings

The **New Britain Grey-headed Goshawk** *Accipiter princeps* is a little-known species restricted to the island of New Britain (off Papua New Guinea), where it inhabits mountain forests at altitudes of between 750 and 1,500 m. This species is thought to be closely related to the Grey-headed Goshawk.

The **Grey Frog Hawk** (Chinese Sparrowhawk) *Accipiter soloensis* breeds in the lowland woods of eastern and southern China, Korea and Taiwan, migrating south for the winter to South-East Asia, the Philippines and Indonesia. It favours wet habitats, such as rice paddies, which support a good supply of its main prey - frogs. It also eats lizards and insects.

Goshawks and relatives

Henst's Goshawk
Status: *Uncommon/ declining/narrow endemic*
Length: *43-58 cm*
Wingspan: *110 cm Resembles the Northern Goshawk (p. 76) in general build, plumage and behaviour*

Meyer's Goshawk
Status: *Rare*
Length: *48-53 cm*
Wingspan: *105 cm Black above, white below. Black phase occurs on New Guinea*

Bürger's Sparrowhawk
Status: *Unknown/ narrow endemic*
Length: *48-53 cm*
Wingspan: *105 cm Dark above, white below. A black phase also occurs*

Henst's Goshawk (Madagascar Goshawk) *Accipiter henstii* is a secretive bird that lives in the humid forests of Madagascar. It feeds on birds and small mammals, and is one of the larger and more powrful of the southern hemisphere goshawks.

Meyer's Goshawk (Papuan Goshawk) *Accipiter meyerianus*, also a shy species, is found in Maluku (the Moluccas), The Solomon Islands, New Britain and is thought to occur in parts of New Guinea.

Bürger's Sparrowhawk (Chestnut-shouldered Goshawk) *Accipiter buergersi* inhabits mountain forests in eastern New Guinea.

All three species are powerful hunters that take their prey in and around forested areas.

Gray's Goshawk
Status: *Unknown/
narrow endemic*
Length: *38 cm*
Wingspan: *75 cm
Slate-grey above,
amber below. The
immature bird (not
shown) is grey-brown
above with white
markings around the
head*

Grey-throated Goshawk
Status: *Unknown/
narrow endemic*
Length: *38 cm*
Wingspan: *75 cm
Grey head and throat.
Dark above, vinous
below*

Gray's Goshawk (Moluccan Barred Sparrowhawk) *Accipiter henicogrammus* is a little-studied species from the Moluccas. It inhabits woodland, where it feeds on medium-sized birds.

The Grey-throated Goshawk (Moluccan Goshawk) *Accipiter griseogularis* is closely related to the Variable Goshawk (p. 80) of which it may be a race.

Even today, these two species are little known, and information about their status and breeding biology is very scanty. This serves to underline the urgent need for field studies of endangered species, especially in tropical forest habitats, which are themselves fast disappearing.

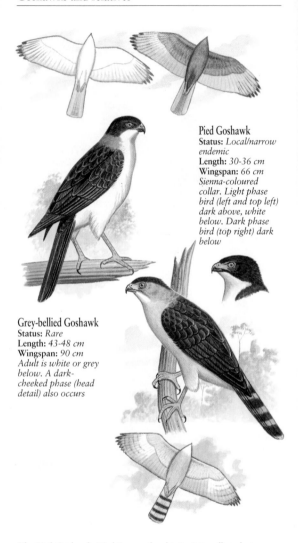

Pied Goshawk
Status: *Local/narrow endemic*
Length: *30-36 cm*
Wingspan: *66 cm Sienna-coloured collar. Light phase bird (left and top left) dark above, white below. Dark phase bird (top right) dark below*

Grey-bellied Goshawk
Status: *Rare*
Length: *43-48 cm*
Wingspan: *90 cm Adult is white or grey below. A dark-cheeked phase (head detail) also occurs*

The **Pied Goshawk** (**Pied Sparrowhawk**) *Accipiter albogularis* occurs in the Solomon Islands, Bismarck Archipelago and Santa Cruz. Although its distribution is limited, the species is highly variable, with at least three recognized colour forms. The light phase, which has pale underparts, occurs with or without a chestnut collar, and the dark phase is slate grey all over. This bird is closely related to the New Caledonia Sparrowhawk (p.95).

The **Grey-bellied Goshawk** *Accipiter poliogaster* is widespread in Guyana, Colombia, Venezuela, Ecuador, Peru, Brazil, Bolivia, Paraguay and Argentina, although it is rare throughout this range. Its preferred habitat is humid lowland forest.

Sparrowhawk
Status: *Common*
Length: *28-38 cm*
Wingspan: *55-70 cm*
Yellow eyes. Adult female (top left; perched right) larger than male (top centre; perched left). Juvenile (top right) has streaks on neck

Levant Sparrowhawk
Status: *Local*
Length: *32-38 cm*
Wingspan: *65-75 cm*
Female (bottom left; perched right) has spots on throat. Male bottom centre; perched left. Juvenile bottom right

The (Northern or Eurasian) Sparrowhawk *Accipiter nisus* is one of Europe's most familiar woodland predators, specializing in small birds, which it ambushes in flight. It is widely distributed from north Africa, through Europe (particularly Scandinavia, the UK and France) to the Pacific coast of Asia, with enclaves in Japan and the Himalaya. Asian birds over-winter in India and South-East Asia. Smaller races with darker plumage are found in Corsica, Sardinia and the Canaries.

The Levant Sparrowhawk *Accipiter brevipes* breeds chiefly in north and west Iran and the USSR, but is also scattered in Turkey and the Balkans. It migrates, mainly over the Bosphorus, to winter in north-east Africa. Its diet is more varied than the Sparrowhawk's.

Shikra
Status: *Common*
Length: *30-36 cm*
Wingspan: *60-70 cm*
*Pale blue-grey above,
with dark wing tips.
Very pale below, with
dark tail bands and
faint throat streak*

Nicobar Shikra
Status: *Local/narrow
endemic*
Length: *26-33 cm*
Wingspan: *60 cm*
*Similar to Shikra, but
paler below. Lacks
the Shikra's dark
wing tips*

The **Shikra** *Accipiter badius* is found throughout most of sub-Saharan Africa (except the Congo basin and the extreme south) and southern Asia. It prefers semi-desert, savanna and cultivated areas: it preys mainly on lizards, large insects and birds, but also takes small rodents, amphibians and even bats. The Shikra builds a stick nest, lined with leaves, in which two to four eggs are laid.

The Nicobar Shikra *Accipiter butleri* is endemic to the Nicobar Islands, where it is the only *Accipiter* hawk. This shy bird is hard to spot, spending much of its time in the tree-tops. Like the Shikra, it feeds on a wide range of animals, with lizards forming a large proportion of prey taken.

In flight, the adult Sharp-shinned Hawk (left) has small, rounded head and square or slightly notched tail

The immature bird (in flight, right), has heavily streaked breast and narrow white terminal tail band

Sharp-shinned Hawk
Status: *Common*
Length: *25-36 cm*
Wingspan: *50-70 cm*
Eye placed centrally on side of head. Similar to Cooper's Hawk but with shorter, squarer tail, smaller head and neck, lighter crown, and narrower white tail-tip

The Sharp-shinned Hawk *Accipiter striatus* is one of North America's commonest hawks and the smallest of the three North American *Accipiters* – the other two being the Northern Goshawk (p. 76) and Cooper's Hawk (p. 90). It is most often seen in the forests of the north and west, although it is present in most areas with large areas of woodland and is a winter visitor to the southern US. Its range extends to the montane forests of Central America, the Carribean, and the Andes mountains as far south as Uruguay.

Sharp-shinned Hawks often migrate in flocks along mountain ridges, passing over in large numbers at locations such as Cape May Point, New Jersey and Hawk Mountain, Pennsylvania.

Sparrowhawks and relatives

In flight, adult Cooper's Hawk (above) shows relatively long tail, short wings and large head

A brownish neck gives the juvenile (above) a hooded appearance. Straight leading edge to wing when soaring

Cooper's Hawk
Status: *Local/possibly declining*
Length: *35-50 cm*
Wingspan: *74-94 cm*
Sexes similar, but female larger

Cooper's Hawk *Accipiter cooperii* favours deciduous woodlands in North America, where it hunts birds and small mammals, usually from a perched position. The species has a more southerly distribution than the Sharp-shinned Hawk (p.89), being found from southern Canada to Florida and northern Mexico. It is uncommon in the east of its range and absent from Central and South America.

Like Sharp-shinned Hawks, these raptors also migrate along mountain ridges, though usually singly or in small groups. The sexes are similar is plumage, but the females are noticeably larger. Male Cooper's Hawks catch mainly small or medium-sized birds, whilst the females tackle larger prey such as grouse.

Rufous-breasted Sparrowhawk
Status: *Local*
Length: *28-33 cm*
Wingspan: *60 cm*
Dark slate-grey above, rufous below

Ovampo Sparrowhawk
Status: *Local/rare*
Length: *30-35 cm*
Wingspan: *75 cm*
Spots on central tail feathers. Relatively long wings. Resembles Shikra (p. 88) but has grey and white barred underparts. Also similar to Gabar Goshawk (p. 75)

The **Rufous-breasted Sparrowhawk** *Accipiter rufiventris* is a fast-flying bird-hunter found in the highland forests of central and southern Africa. It has been seen at altitudes of over 3,600 m in the mountains of Ethiopia. These birds build small nests, usually in coniferous trees, and are very energetic in defending their territory against intruders. Otherwise, they are quite shy birds which are hard to observe in their dense woodland habitat.

The **Ovampo Sparrowhawk** *Accipiter ovampensis* is a shy bird found on the dry savannas of central and southern Africa (though absent from the Congo basin and Cape region). It hunts birds to the size of small doves, as well as insects and small mammals.

Little Sparrowhawk
Status: *Local*
Length: *23-28 cm*
Wingspan: *48 cm*
Like miniature male African Goshawk (p. 78), but has white rump. Slate-grey above

Red-thighed Sparrowhawk
Status: *Local*
Length: *25-31 cm*
Wingspan: *53 cm*
Closely resembles Little Sparrowhawk, but chest and upper breast are rufous

Chestnut-bellied Sparrowhawk
Status: *Local*
Length: *30-40 cm*
Wingspan: *70 cm*
Slate-grey above, sepia below, with rust-coloured flanks. Relatively short wings and heavily barred underparts

The **(African) Little Sparrowhawk** *Accipiter minullus*, Africa's smallest hawk, is found in woodland and scrub throughout most of sub-Saharan Africa, from sea-level right up to 2,000 m. This agile bird's prey comprises small song birds, insects and reptiles. It is a relatively tame species and can often be approached quite closely before it is disturbed and flies away.

The Red-thighed Sparrowhawk *Accipiter erythropus* lives in dense forests in Uganda (especially the Bwamba Forest), Gambia, Cameroon, Congo, and south to Angola.

The Chestnut-bellied Sparrowhawk *Accipiter castanilius* is a secretive forest hawk from Nigeria, Cameroon and Congo.

Japanese Sparrowhawk
Status: *Local*
Length: *23-28 cm*
Wingspan: *50 cm*
Dark above, pale below. Male bird (right and in flight) has amber breast

The female bird (left) is barred white and brown beneath. Lacks obvious throat streak

Besra
Status: *Common*
Length: *24-35 cm*
Wingspan: *56 cm*
Resembles Shikra (p. 88) but has heavier throat-streak. Brown above, barred below. Female (shown here) has amber-brown on breast and sides

The Japanese Sparrowhawk *Accipiter gularis* breeds in eastern China, Japan and the extreme south-east of the USSR. A close relative of the Besra, it is the smallest South-East Asian *Accipiter*, and an active predator of small and medium-sized birds. These birds migrate in dense flocks to their winter quarters in South-East Asia.

The Besra (Sparrowhawk) *Accipiter virgatus* is found in the mountain forests of India, Sri Lanka, southern Asia, the Philippines and parts of Indonesia. It reaches heights of up to 3,000 m on some Himalayan slopes.

The two above species are very closely related and are often hard to distinguish in the field, particularly when immature.

Bi-coloured Sparrowhawk
Status: *Locally common*
Length: *33-38 cm*
Wingspan: *70 cm*

Silver-grey with bright rust-coloured thighs. Barred phase occurs in Chile and Argentina

The Bi-coloured Sparrowhawk typically hunts for small birds from a vantage point in a forest clearing

Gundlach's Hawk
Status: *Narrow endemic/rare/declining*
Length: *40-50 cm*
Wingspan: *90 cm*
Rounded tail. Similar in build to Cooper's Hawk (p.90), but with more powerful legs and feet

The Bi-coloured Sparrowhawk *Accipiter bicolor* replaces Cooper's Hawk in South America, from southern Mexico throughout most of the continent. It is found at altitudes of up to 2,000 m in open woodland with scattered clearings: it is often found in secondary forest (woodland that has regenerated after clearance).

Gundlach's Hawk (Cuban Hawk) *Accipiter gundlachi* is a rare, secretive bird found in swamps, coastal woods and hills in Cuba. Its habitat is threatened by deforestation.

Both the above species are thought to be closely related to Cooper's Hawk (p.90), and are similar in build, though they have different plumage patterns.

Blue and Grey Sparrowhawk
Status: *Unknown/*
narrow endemic
Length: *30-38 cm*
Wingspan: *70 cm*
Slate-coloured above

Imitator Sparrowhawk
Status: *Rare/narrow*
endemic
Length: *28-33 cm*
Wingspan: *55-65 cm*

New Caledonia Sparrowhawk
Status: *Rare/narrow*
endemic
Length: *31-36 cm*
Wingspan: *70 cm*
Black above, white
below with black
throat and
barred chest

The Blue and Grey Sparrowhawk *Accipiter luteoschistaceus* is known only from New Britain (Papua New Guinea), where it lives in mountain forests.

The Imitator Sparrowhawk *Accipiter imitator* is confined to rainforest in the northern Solomon Islands (Choiseul and Santa Isabel), and Papua New Guinea (Bougainville). Little is known about its habits. White-breasted and black phases are known to occur: these may be confused with the two phases of the Pied Goshawk (p. 86).

The rare New Caledonia Sparrowhawk *Accipiter haplochrous* is another endemic, found only on New Caledonia, where it feeds mainly on birds in the dense forests.

Spot-tailed Sparrowhawk
Status: *Local/narrow endemic*
Length: *25-28 cm*
Wingspan: *50 cm*
Slate-blue above, chestnut below. Tail black with white spots. Could be confused in the field with the other endemic sparrow-hawks of Sulawesi (see p. 98)

Black-mantled Goshawk
Status: *Uncommon/narrow endemic*
Length: *33-38 cm*
Wingspan: *70 cm*
Black head with wide sienna-coloured collar and sienna underparts

The **Spot-tailed Sparrowhawk** *Accipiter trinotatus* is endemic to Sulawesi. Its haunts are virgin forests (to about 1,400 m) and mangrove swamps, with reptiles probably forming a large part of its diet. This bird tends to stay hidden in thick forest cover and is therefore difficult to observe. However, its characteristic call – a repeated "hee" note – often gives away its presence.

The Black-mantled Goshawk (Sparrowhawk) *Accipiter melanochlamys* is an inhabitant of New Guinea and New Britain, where it is found in mountain forests at altitudes of between 1,500 and 3,500 m. Little is known of its general biology, though it is rather rare and has a limited distribution.

Madagascar Sparrowhawk
Status: *Uncommon/
narrow endemic*
Length: *34-38 cm*
Wingspan: *65 cm*
*Brown above, barred
below. Similar in
appearance and
behaviour to the
Northern
Sparrowhawk (p. 87).
Also resembles
Henst's Goshawk (p.
84), but smaller*

Frances' Sparrowhawk
Status: *Local/narrow
endemic*
Length: *27-33 cm*
Wingspan: *58 cm*
*Male (pictured) grey
above, white or sandy
below. Female
browner above,
heavily barred below*

The **Madagascar Sparrowhawk** *Accipiter madagascariensis* is found
only in Madagascar, where it favours relatively dry woodland habitats
up to about 1,000 m. This species appears to behave in much the same
way as the Northern Sparrowhawk, which it closely resembles, both in
size and plumage.

Frances' Sparrowhawk *Accipiter francesii* ocurrs in similar country
in Madagascar and the nearby Comoros, but is also found at higher
elevations together with Henst's Goshawk (p. 84). This relatively tame
bird usually hunts from a perch, catching its prey of reptiles (including
chamaeleons), insects and birds on the ground. It builds the typical
hawk nest of sticks, sited high in a forest tree.

Sparrowhawks and relatives

Dwarf Sparrowhawk
Status: *Rare/narrow endemic*
Length: *23-26 cm*
Wingspan: *46 cm*
Slate-blue above, chestnut below. Tail brown. Sexes of similar size

Vinous-breasted Sparrowhawk
Status: *Local/narrow endemic*
Length: *27-33 cm*
Wingspan: *57 cm*
Slate-blue above, chestnut below. Tail has grey bands. Grey on throat and thighs. Female distinctly larger than male

The Dwarf Sparrowhawk *Accipiter nanus,* also known as the Sulawesi Little Sparrowhawk or Small Sparrowhawk, is found at altitudes of between 900 and 1,800 m in the mountain forests of Sulawesi.

The Vinous-breasted Sparrowhawk *Accipiter rhodogaster* also inhabits mainland Sulawesi, as well as the nearby islands of Butung, Muna and Peleng. Male Vinous-breasted Sparrowhawks are difficult to tell apart from Dwarf sparrowhawks in the field, but females are easier to distinguish due to their larger size. It is found from sea-level (often in mangroves) up to about 650 m, where it lives in forests and groves of trees, and occasionally on the outskirts of villages. Both of the above feed on insects and small birds.

Moluccan Collared Sparrowhawk
Status: *Rare/narrow endemic*
Length: *28-34 cm*
Wingspan: *60 cm*
Chestnut below, usually with light grey barring

Chestnut collar. Although variable in plumage, it usually has some chestnut colouring on breast

New Britain Collared Sparrowhawk
Status: *Rare and threatened/narrow endemic*
Length: *27-34 cm*
Wingspan: *58 cm*
Chestnut collar but not underparts

Light grey below. Tail sometimes shows shallow notch

The (Grey) **Moluccan Collared Sparrowhawk** *Accipiter erythrauchen* is found from sea-level to about 1,400 m in Maluku (the Moluccas), on the islands of Morotai, Halmahera, Bacan, Obi, Buru, Ambon and Seram. This colourful hawk is rather variable in plumage, sometimes being faintly barred below, and sometimes grey. Little is known of its ecology, though it is thought to eat mainly small birds.

The **New Britain Collared Sparrowhawk** *Accipiter brachyurus* lives only in the rainforests of New Britain, where it is found from sea-level to about 900 m, The two above species, and the Blue and Grey Sparrowhawk (p.95) are thought to be closely related to the Collared Sparrowhawk (p. 79).

99

Sparrowhawks and relatives

Tiny Sparrowhawk
Status: *Local and rare*
Length: *22-25 cm*
Wingspan: *45 cm*
Barred olive-brown below

Orange feet and orange-red eyes. This diminutive hawk is an agile forest hunter

Semi-collared Sparrowhawk
Status: *Local and rare/threatened*
Length: *30 cm*
Wingspan: *57 cm*
Pale collar

White below with amber bars. Wings appear paler in flight than those of Tiny Sparrowhawk

The Tiny Sparrowhawk *Accipiter superciliosus* of Central and South America is the world's smallest hawk. It lives in woodland and open forest from southeastern Nicaragua to east Peru and Ecuador, the Guianas, Brazil, Paraguay and northern Argentina. In some areas this species specializes in catching hummingbirds: it waits at their courtship grounds and ambushes them during their displays.

The Semi-collared Sparrowhawk (American Collared Sparrowhawk) *Accipiter collaris* is seldom seen, and found only in humid or wet forest in parts of Colombia, Ecuador, Venezuela and Peru. Its distribution in these areas is very patchy and its true status is still uncertain.

Family Accipitridae (part). 56 species in 14 genera

A typical buzzard in soaring flight shows broad, rounded wings and a fan-shaped tail

Key features

Medium-sized to large
Long, broad wings
Sexes similar

Buteo *hawks have modest-sized bills and rounded heads*

This group of raptors is both large and diverse. Most of its members feed on mammals and reptiles, usually pouncing on their prey while it is on the ground. Females of most species are slightly larger than males, but the sexes are similar in plumage, which can be shades of brown and chestnut, or black and white, or a combination of the two.

The true buzzards of the genus *Buteo* (most of which are rather confusingly known as hawks) make up just under half of the group, with 26 species. These medium-sized raptors have a bill and feet of moderate size and a short, fan-shaped tail. Many are variable in plumage, with dark, light and rufous forms predominating in different regions. They have long, broad wings and typically soar in circles for long periods; some species can hang on the breeze, and hover.

The next largest genus of the group, with ten species, is *Leucopternis*. The birds of this genus are found in tropical Central and South America, where they specialize in hunting amongst rainforest trees, or alongside rivers and clearings. They have broad, but rather short wings, and striking white, or black and white plumage.

Buzzards and relatives

Family Accipitridae (part). 56 species in 14 genera

In flight, the Harpy Eagle resembles a giant goshawk

The Philippine Eagle's deep and heavy bill allows it to tear the flesh of large forest mammals, such as monkeys and small deer

The five species of the genus *Buteogallus* – the black hawks and their relatives – are also tropical American in distribution, though one, the Common Black Hawk, just penetrates into the USA. They have very broad wings and short, square tails. Most have dark plumage.

The Grasshopper Buzzard and its three relatives of the genus *Butastur* are dainty birds, with small bills, long wings and tails, and long scaly legs with weak feet. The Grasshopper Buzzard itself is an African resident; the others all occur in southern and South-East Asia.

The two rare solitary eagles (genus *Harpyhaliaetus*) live in the tropical forests of South America. They are large, powerful hawks of eagle-like proportions, with dark plumage, long wings and short tails.

The nine other species in this group are each assigned to their own genus, having no close relatives. These species include in their number the rare Philippine Eagle and the two harpy eagles (genera *Harpyopsis* and *Harpia*). These giant forest hunters, which are even more massive than the solitary eagles, have long tails and short, broad wings.

The Lizard Buzzard resembles the Gabar Goshawk (p. 75), but has longer, more rounded wings

Lizard Buzzard
Status: *Locally common*
Length: *35-38 cm*
Wingspan: *90 cm Thick-set in appearance. Pale grey with white rump*

The Lizard Buzzard *Kaupifalco monogrammicus* has a wide distribution in sub-Saharan Africa, where its preferred habitats are open park-like country, savannas, cultivated areas, woodland edges, and coconut plantations. Slow and graceful in flight, it swoops down from the air or from a perch to catch small mammals, reptiles, and large insects.

Distinctive long, wedge-shaped tail (longer than head and body)

Long-tailed Hawk
Status: *Uncommon*
Length: *56-58 cm*
Wingspan: *90 cm Slate-coloured above, chestnut below. Dark brown wings, white rump*

The (African) Long-tailed Hawk *Urotriorchis macrourus* is a secretive tree-top hunter found in the tropical forests of west and central Africa. It feeds on birds and rodents and hardly ever alights on the ground, a trait which has given rise to its local name - "leopard of the air". Its stronghold is in the tropical forests of the Congo basin, though it is also known from Uganda's Bwamba Forest.

103

Buzzard relatives

The Grasshopper Buzzard appears harrier-like in flight, with its ringed tail and brown plumage

Grasshopper Buzzard
Status: *Locally common*
Length: *40-43 cm*
Wingspan: *100 cm*
Grey-brown above, amber-brown below. Chestnut wings

Rufous-winged Buzzard
Status: *Local*
Length: *35-40 cm*
Wingspan: *95 cm*
Slender chestnut wings and tail (square-cut). Pale below

In flight, this buzzard's pointed wings and square-cut tail are visible

The Grasshopper Buzzard *Butastur rufipennis* breeds just south of the Sahara, in a belt that stretches from from Senegal to Somalia, but spends the months from November to March in northern Uganda, north-east Tanzania and eastern Kenya (where it is common in the Tsavo National park throughout December and January). These sociable birds may occur in flocks of up to 100 individuals. They feed mainly on insects, but also take small mammals.

The Rufous-winged Buzzard *Butastur liventer* lives in Burma, Thailand, southern Borneo and parts of Indonesia (including Java and Sulawesi). It is found in wooded and open country, often near rivers and rice-paddies, and its diet includes crabs, reptiles and frogs.

Pale wings with dark markings. Tail has dark subterminal band

White-eyed Buzzard
Status: *Locally common*
Length: *40-43 cm*
Wingspan: *100 cm*
Throat is striped black at sides and centre. Pale wing patch.

Grey-faced Buzzard
Status: *Locally common*
Length: *40-45 cm*
Wingspan: *105 cm*
White throat is striped grey at sides and centre. Tail has three dark bands

Slender, pointed wings are pale below. Breast is brownish

The **White-eyed Buzzard** *Butastur teesa* is present in Pakistan, India, Assam and Burma, reaching about 900 m in the Himalaya: it becomes rarer in the south of its range, and is absent from Sri Lanka. It commonly hunts from a perch in dry, open country, taking large insects, rodents and reptiles. This somewhat sluggish bird is said to be quite tame, and often perches on telegraph poles. It is noisy during the breeding season, the female having a distinctive mewing cry.

The Grey-faced Buzzard *Butastur indicus* breeds in wooded areas of eastern China and Japan. In the winter, flocks of thousands of these birds migrate through Japan to the Kurile Islands and south China, where they are often seen on paddy-fields.

Juvenile (below) has a rather speckled appearance. The breast is heavily streaked

Adult (above and below) has black head, body and wing coverts. Black below but for white patches at base of outer primaries

Common Black Hawk
Status: *Local*
Length: *53 cm*
Wingspan: *127 cm*

Great Black Hawk
Status: *Locally common*
Length: *55 cm*
Wingspan: *132 cm*
Powerful bill and feet

Broad wings and short, square tail visible in flight

The **Common Black Hawk** *Buteogallus anthracinus* occurs locally in parts of Texas, New Mexico and Arizona. Its range extends southwards through Mexico to Panama and north-west Peru, taking in Cuba and some other Caribbean Islands. Favouring coastal lowland savanna and wooded streams and rivers, it hunts from a perch for fish, frogs, reptiles, birds and small mammals. This bird also takes crabs and crayfish, opening up their carapaces with its sharply hooked bill.

The Great Black Hawk *Buteogallus urubitinga* is similar to the Common Black Hawk, though larger and less gregarious. The ranges of the two species overlaps in much of northern South America, but the former also occurs in the east, as far south as Paraguay.

The Mangrove Black Hawk is shown in flight (left)

Mangrove Black Hawk
Status: *Local*
Length: *53 cm*
Wingspan: *127 cm*
*Amber-brown
secondaries*

Rufous Crab Hawk
Status: *Local*
Length: *45 cm*
Wingspan: *110 cm*
*Differs from the black
hawks by its brighter
plumage, smaller size
and shorter tail*

*Note the narrow
barring on breast and
belly. Notched tail*

The Mangrove Black Hawk (Pacific Black Hawk) *Buteogallus subtilis* replaces the Common Black Hawk in the mangrove swamps of the Pacific coast, from El Salvador to southern Ecuador. It feeds mainly on crabs and fish.

The Rufous Crab Hawk *Buteogallus aequinoctialis* lives along the Atlantic coast of northern and eastern South America, from Venezuela to south-east Brazil. It feeds almost exclusively on crabs, which it hunts from branches overhanging shallow creeks, mainly in mangrove swamps. In the field, this bird may be confused with the Savanna Hawk (p. 108), though it is dumpier, has shorter legs, and a much more limited coastal range.

Note the long legs, reaching towards the tip of the tail. Distinctive coppery plumage

Savanna Hawk
Status: *Common*
Length: *55 cm*
Wingspan: *130 cm*
Bright plumage. Long legs and short tail. Long, broad wings

The **Savanna Hawk** *Buteogallus meridionalis* has a very distinctive bright rufous plumage and resembles the other members of its genus only in general build. It favours savanna and similar open country with scattered trees, often close to marshland, ponds or rivers. This bird hunts a wide range of animals, including reptiles, amphibians, small mammals and insects, usually from a low perch such as a post or hummock. It frequently glides close to the ground, prospecting for prey, and sometimes follows grass fires, picking off animals disturbed by the blaze. The Savanna Hawk's long legs help it to move about easily on the ground when it is in search of prey amongst coarse grass and tussocks.

Distinctive in flight, with black head and tip to tail. Belly and wings are barred black

Barred Hawk
Status: *Local*
Length: *47 cm*
Wingspan: *112 cm*
Cere orange, eyes dark blue

Slate-coloured Hawk
Status: *Threatened*
Length: *44 cm*
Wingspan: *105 cm*
Black tail with white band and tip

The Slate-coloured Hawk is shown in flight (right)

The Barred Hawk *Leucopternis princeps* occurs in mountain forests between about 1,200 and 1,500 m from Costa Rica, south to northern Ecuador. This hawk feeds mainly on reptiles. It is not easily observed, partly because of its habitat, but also since it is local or rare over much of its range. Like several of its relatives, it is at risk from habitat loss.

The Slate-coloured Hawk *Leucopternis schistacea* of northern central South America (particularly the the Amazon region) is a bird of swamps, forested streams and river-banks. It usually hunts from a perch for its prey of snakes and amphibians. The species is threatened by habitat loss.

White Hawk
Status: *Local*
Length: *46 cm*
Wingspan: *110 cm*
Black sub-terminal tail band. Wings have black tips and bars

Black-faced Hawk
Status: *Local*
Length: *35 cm*
Wingspan: *85 cm*
Black mask. Orange cere

The **White Hawk** *Leucopternis albicollis* inhabits mixed forest from southern Mexico through Central America to the southern Amazon basin. It is often seen soaring above the trees singly or in small groups, and is easily identified, being the only mainly-white hawk. White Hawks build twig nests, lined with fresh leaves, high in tall trees.

The Black-faced Hawk *Leucopternis melanops* occurs north of the Amazon, to southern Venezuela, eastern Colombia and Ecuador. It prefers savanna, where it is often spotted near water holes, but is also found in mangroves. Like most other species in this genus, the Black-faced Hawk feeds on reptiles, small mammals, birds and insects.

In flight, the black tail with its median white band is clearly visible

Plumbeous Hawk
Status: *Rare*
Length: *35 cm*
Wingspan: *85 cm*
Small and stocky in build. Black wings. Slate-grey plumage. Orange cere, bright red eyes

Semi-plumbeous Hawk
Status: *Locally common*
Length: *34 cm*
Wingspan: *82 cm*
Small and stocky in build. Slate-grey above, white below

Underparts white, except for tail, which is black with a central white band

The **Plumbeous Hawk** *Leucopternis plumbea* has a restricted range in Panama, western Colombia, north-west Peru and western Ecuador.

The **Semi-plumbeous Hawk** *Leucopternis semiplumbea* has a similar distribution to the above species, but reaches further north into Central America through Costa Rica and Nicaragua to Honduras. Its favoured habitat is wet primary forest, where it is one of the commonest hawks. It is a vocal bird, uttering loud, whistling calls. This species is much more common than the darker Plumbeous Hawk. However, both species are easily overlooked because of their small size and preference for densely forested country.

Hawks

Very pale undersides of wings and body, with dark tip to tail

White-browed Hawk
Status: *Local*
Length: *34 cm*
Wingspan: *82 cm*
Dark above with white eyebrows. Tail black with median white band. Dark upperside contrasts sharply with pale underside

White-necked Hawk
Status: *Rare/narrow endemic*
Length: *35 cm*
Wingspan: *85 cm*
Face, head and neck light grey. Tail white with black band

Similar, when in flight, to the larger Black Mantled Hawk (p. 113), but note black tip to tail

The **White-browed Hawk** *Leucopternis kuhli* inhabits the southern Amazon basin of Brazil and eastern Peru. Though not as rare as some of its close relatives, this species has been little studied, partly because it is difficult to observe in its densely forested habitat.

The White-necked Hawk *Leucopternis lacernulata* is found in the Atlantic lowland forests of Brazil. Threatened by habitat loss, this rare bird remains rather obscure, but it is thought to include invertebrates in its diet.

In flight, the Grey-backed Hawk's white tail with its wide subterminal black band is clearly visible

Grey-backed Hawk
Status: *Threatened/ narrow endemic*
Length: *45 cm*
Wingspan: *108 cm*
Dark grey above, white below

Mantled Hawk
Status: *Local*
Length: *44 cm*
Wingspan: *105 cm*

Best distinguished from the similar White-necked Hawk by the tail pattern

The **Grey-backed Hawk** *Leucopternis occidentalis* is a little known species of western Ecuador and north-west Peru where it is threatened by deforestation. This bird has the most restricted distribution of all the *Leucopternis* hawks. It is therefore of particular concern that it seems to have declined markedly in recent years.

The Mantled Hawk *Leucopternis polionota* is scarce in the Atlantic forests of eastern Brazil, south-east Paraguay and parts of northern Argentina, but is seen regularly in Brazil's Iguazù National Park.

Juvenile Black-collared Hawk is shown in flight (left)

The adult bird (right) has black-tipped wings and tail

Black-collared Hawk
Status: *Locally common*
Length: *48 cm*
Wingspan: *115 cm*
Chestnut plumage. White head with black crescent on chin. Bill strongly curved. Long legs, heavy feet

The **Black-collared Hawk** (**Fishing Buzzard**) *Bursarellus nigricollis* is a distinctive species with a highly specialized lifestyle. Like the Osprey (p. 14), it feeds on fish, and though it occasionally catches its prey in an Osprey-like dive into shallow water, it more commonly snatches fish out of the water with its talons, and so avoids wetting its feathers. Its feet have rough spicules beneath to help the bird grip its slippery prey. It sometimes takes other prey, such as reptiles, snails and small mammals. This species favours marshy habitats, coastal lagoons and other wetlands from southern Mexico south to Brazil, Paraguay and northern Argentina. Often seen perched on a prominent branch or telegraph post.

Wings long and
broad. Tail rather
short and rounded.
Often soars at great
height

Black-chested Buzzard Eagle
Status: *Local/
unknown*
Length: *66 cm*
Wingspan: *158 cm*

Ragged neck feathers
and deeply hooked
bill. Partially feathered
legs

The **Black-chested Buzzard Eagle** *Geranoaetus melanoleucus* is well-named, being intermediate in appearance and habits between a buzzard and a true eagle. Its distribution roughly follows the line of the Andes, from Venezuela to Tierra del Fuego. In ecology, it more closely resembles an eagle, preferring mountains and plains, and hunting from high, soaring flight, mainly for medium-sized mammals and carrion. This bird often spends long periods perched on a vantage point, such as a rock, on the lookout for suitable prey.

Like the true eagles, Black-chested Buzzard Eagles build large nests from thick twigs, often using the same nest year after year and enlarging it each season.

115

Hawks

Harris' Hawk
Status: *Locally common*
Length: *52 cm*
Wingspan: *115 cm*
Chestnut shoulders and thighs. Sexes similar, but female larger

Black tail with white base and tip

Harris' Hawk *Parabuteo unicinctus* is a wide-ranging species found over semi-arid scrub from the extreme south of the US, through Mexico and Central America as far south as central Chile and Argentina. Harris' Hawks sometimes hunt in groups and large flocks may be seen in the autumn.

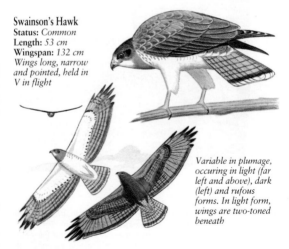

Swainson's Hawk
Status: *Common*
Length: *53 cm*
Wingspan: *132 cm*
Wings long, narrow and pointed, held in V in flight

Variable in plumage, occuring in light (far left and above), dark (left) and rufous forms. In light form, wings are two-toned beneath

Swainson's Hawk *Buteo swainsoni* is a frequent summer visitor to the open plains, prairies and semi-deserts of western North America, wintering mostly in southern South America. It hunts for small mammals, insects and birds from a perch or from soaring, kite-like flight. Sometimes follows tractors and mowing machines to catch disturbed insects, birds and small rodents.

Ferruginous Hawk
Status: *Common*
Length: *58 cm*
Wingspan: *143 cm*
Rust-coloured back, shoulders and leg-feathers. Head pale

In flight (juvenile left, adult right), wings appear broad and long. Soars with wings in a shallow V

The Ferruginous Hawk *Buteo regalis* is a bird of western North America, and is particularly common in dry, open country from north Texas to southern Oregon. In winter it migrates south to northern Mexico. This shy species feeds mainly on ground squirrels and jack rabbits which it captures by swooping down from the air or from a convenient perch.

White-tailed Hawk
Status: *Locally common*
Length: *50 cm*
Wingspan: *130 cm*
Large with pointed wings

Resembles Swainson's Hawk (p. 116) in flight and silhouette. Soars with wings in V

The White-tailed Hawk *Buteo albicaudatus* has a split distribution in the Americas. From the coastal prairies and chaparral of southern Texas it extends down to northern South America, and then reappears in central south-east South America. It eats reptiles, insects, birds and mammals, caught from gliding or hovering flight, or from a perch. Sometimes gathers near forest fires to catch fleeing animals.

117

True buzzards and *Buteo* hawks

Red-shouldered Hawk
Status: *Common*
Length: *43 cm*
Wingspan: *102 cm*
The western race (far left) is more rufous below. Eastern race (left and in flight) is smaller and paler

Crescent-shaped wing bars. Shows red shoulder patches when perched

Juvenile western bird (above left), juvenile eastern (above right)

The Red-shouldered Hawk *Buteo lineatus* is found in the USA from the Great Lakes south and east to the Texas coast, and also on the Caribbean coast of northern Mexico. An isolated population exists in coastal California. Its prefers wet woodland and savanna where it feeds on birds, mammals, amphibians and reptiles. Two races are recognized.

Broad-winged Hawk
Status: *Common*
Length: *37 cm*
Wingspan: *86 cm*
Dark brown above, rufous below. Adult (perched left) has dark tail with broad white band. Juvenile shown perched right

Flies on flat wings. Wings show dark rear border below (adult). Wing tips are distinctly pointed

The Broad-winged Hawk *Buteo platypterus* is found mainly in the North American forests east of the Great Plains, but is also present further north and east to Alberta. Commonly flies down rapidly from its woodland perch to capture its prey of small mammals, birds, frogs, snakes and insects. This bird is seen in large numbers on migration.

118

Shown left is the eastern form. Note the rufous tail

The darkest form (above) is known as Harlan's Hawk. Note the grey tail. Shown left is the dark form

Red-tailed Hawk
Status: *Common*
Length: *50 cm*
Wingspan: *125 cm*
Dark patches on underwings

Shown in flight (above) is adult eastern form

In flight (above), juvenile eastern form shows pale wing patches

Adult dark form in flight (above)

The Red-tailed Hawk *Buteo jamaicensis,* North America's commonest hawk, is found over the entire continent except the extreme north. Its range extends southwards as far as Panama and the West Indies: northern populations are migratory, wintering in the southern US or in Central America.

Red-tailed Hawks are highly variable in plumage, with several different forms recognized. They are found in a wide range of habitats, from forest and woodland, to prairie and semi-desert, where they feed mainly on rodents, though they will take fish, insects and even carrion. These birds often perch in prominent positions, such as high in trees, or on top of tall poles.

True buzzards and *Buteo* hawks

Zone-tailed Hawk
Status: *Uncommon*
Length: *51 cm*
Wingspan: *130 cm*
Two-toned underwing

The **Zone-tailed Hawk** *Buteo albonotatus* is found in the hills and canyons of Texas, New Mexico and Arizona, south through Mexico to Paraguay and Bolivia. This hawk is sometimes confused with the Turkey Vulture, which it may mimic in order to get close to its prey, indeed, the two species sometimes fly together when prospecting for food. It feeds mainly on reptiles, rodents, fish and frogs.

Short-tailed Hawk
Status: *Local*
Length: *40 cm*
Wingspan: *93 cm*
Dark phase (far left and below) is dark below; light phase (left) is pale below

White-throated Hawk
Status: *Local*
Length: *40 cm*
Wingspan: *92 cm*
Amber-brown streaks on neck and thighs

The **Short-tailed Hawk** *Buteo brachyurus*, a hunter of small birds, occurs in wooded lowlands and hilly country from central Mexico south to Paraguay, Argentina and southern Brazil, reaching about 2,000 m in the Andes. Above this altitude, it is replaced by the White-throated Hawk *Buteo albigula*. The latter is also found down to sea-level in Chile.

White-rumped Hawk
Status: *Unknown*
Length: *38 cm*
Wingspan: *80 cm*
Black plumage with white rump. Rufous thighs. Tail has two white bars

Grey Hawk
Status: *Local*
Length: *42 cm*
Wingspan: *90 cm*
Long-tailed and Accipiter-like. Adult (far left) is grey above and grey-barred below. Juvenile (left) is rufous, with several bars on its tail

In flight, adults (above) show white U at base of tail. Juvenile (below) has streaked breast

The **White-rumped Hawk (Rufous-thighed Hawk)** *Buteo leucorrhous* is a dark forest hawk found in mountain foothills from Colombia and Venezuela to south-east Brazil and Paraguay. Little is known about this species, which is occasionally glimpsed as it soars over the forest canopy.

The **Grey Hawk** *Buteo nitidus* is rare in southern Arizona, where there are thought to be about 50 pairs, and in the extreme south of Texas. The main part of its range extends southwards from Mexico, through Central America to most of northern and eastern South America. This active predator hunts mainly lizards and small birds in open woodland, often close to water.

True buzzards and *Buteo* hawks

Roadside Hawk
Status: *Locally common*
Length: *36 cm*
Wingspan: *75 cm*
Adult (far left and in flight) has a dark breast. Juvenile (left) has a streaked upper breast

Small and chunky in build. Dark bib. Long banded tail and long legs

The **Roadside Hawk** *Buteo magnirostris* is a bird of open woodland, savanna and scrub from eastern Mexico to Argentina and south-east Brazil. It takes its name from its habit of perching in the open, often on roadside poles or wires. It feeds mainly on insects and reptiles but will also take small mammals and birds. It is often attracted to grass fires to pick off animals fleeing the flames.

Rufous-tailed Hawk
Status: *Rare*
Length: *48 cm*
Wingspan: *120 cm*
Similar to Red-tailed Hawk, but darker

The adult Rufous-tailed Hawk is shown in flight (right)

The **Rufous-tailed Hawk** *Buteo ventralis* is a little-studied species found in the Andean regions of central Chile and Argentina, south to Tierra del Fuego. It favours woods and forested slopes. This species is similar to the Red-tailed Hawk (p. 119) to which it is closely related.

Red-backed Hawk
Status: *Local*
Length: *50 cm*
Wingspan: *122 cm*
Red-backed and Variable Hawks are very similar in appearance

The grey phase of the Red-backed Hawk (right and above) is slate-grey above, with a brown patch and pale underparts

Variable Hawk
Status: *Local*
Length: *53 cm*
Wingspan: *133 cm*
The grey phase male (left and below) is grey-black above and below: the female has a brown back

Dark chest, barred belly. Tail has subterminal black band

The Red-backed Hawk (Red-backed Buzzard) *Buteo polyosoma* and the Variable Hawk *Buteo poecilochrous* (also known as Gurney's Buzzard and the Puna Hawk) are two very similar species found in the Andean region of South America. The Red-backed has the wider distribution, being found from Colombia south to Tierra del Fuego. It often hunts guinea pigs in grassland areas.

The Variable Hawk is found mainly in the Peruvian Andes where it reaches higher altitudes (to about 5,500 m) than the Red-backed Hawk. It is slightly larger and more powerful than the above species, and has longer wings. It inhabits rocky country with wooded hills.

True buzzards and *Buteo* hawks

Ridgway's Hawk
Status: *Rare/narrow endemic*
Length: *35 cm*
Wingspan: *73 cm*

This bird is slightly smaller and paler than the Roadside Hawk (p. 112). Wings are barred brown and white

Ridgway's Hawk *Buteo ridgwayi* is found only in Hispaniola. It may already be extinct in mainland Haiti and its habitat is rapidly disappearing in the Dominican Republic. It is a bird of open woodland, favouring lowland locations. Ridgway's Hawks feed mainly on lizards, small mammals and birds.

Galápagos Hawk
Status: *Rare/narrow endemic*
Length: *50 cm*
Wingspan: *115 cm*
Dark brown plumage. Barred tail

Galápagos Hawk has rather drab all-brown plumage

The Galápagos Hawk *Buteo galapagoensis* is very tame, like many other animals found on the Galápagos Islands. It is the only hawk on the islands, where its population stands at only around 130 pairs. One unusual feature of this species is that it is polyandrous, each female pairing with more than one male, sometimes as many as five. The males all share in defending the territory, in mating and in feeding the young. They feed on small birds and lizards.

One of the smallest Buteos. The dark phase (not shown) is uniformly dark below

Hawaiian Hawk
Status: *Locally common*
Length: *41-46 cm*
Wingspan: *100 cm*
Occurs in two colour phases. White phase (shown here) is mainly white with sandy wings and tail

The Hawaiian Hawk *Buteo solitarius* is restricted to Hawaii (chiefly to the island of Hawaii itself), where numbers have increased slightly following protection of the species. This rare bird prefers light woodland at altitudes of between 600 and 1,500 m. Introduced rats now make up its main prey.

Madagascar Buzzard
Status: *Common/ narrow endemic*
Length: *40-43 cm*
Wingspan: *95 cm*

Whiter below than Mountain Buzzard and with shorter wings

The Madagascar Buzzard *Buteo brachypterus* is similar in appearance to the Mountain Buzzard (p. 126), which it replaces on Madagascar. It is the only *Buteo* on the island, and is common in wooded and more open areas to about 2,000 m. It takes a wide range of prey, including mammals, reptiles, amphibians and insects. It is the commonest raptor on Madagascar, and can often be seen soaring in wide circles, scrutinizing the ground below.

True buzzards and *Buteo* hawks

Eurasian Buzzard
Status: *Common*
Length: *51-57 cm*
Wingspan: *113-128 cm*
Broad wings and relatively short tail

Often seen soaring in circles over pasture and woods with wings held in a shallow V. Sometimes hovers heavily

The Eurasian Buzzard's plumage is highly variable. The pale form is shown left

Mountain Buzzard
Status: *Local*
Length: *40-43 cm*
Wingspan: *98 cm*

Similar to Eurasian Buzzard, but smaller. Rufous only on lower belly and thighs

The Eurasian Buzzard (Common Buzzard) *Buteo buteo* is Europe's commonest raptor after the Kestrel. Its range extends from the Cape Verde Islands and Azores in the west, through much of Europe and northern Asia, to Japan. In Europe, it is particularly common in Portugal, Germany, Switzerland and Austria; British populations are restricted to the more wooded west and north. Occasionally utters a cat-like mewing call. Feeds mainly on small mammals, but occasionally take birds, reptiles, amphibians, insects and even earthworms.

The (African) Mountain Buzzard *Buteo oreophilus* inhabits mountain forests (between 1,800 and 4,500 m) in east-central Africa, and lower-level forests and plantations in south-east Africa.

Rough-legged Buzzard
Status: *Local
(populations fluctuate)*
Length: *50-60 cm*
Wingspan: *120-150 cm
Slightly larger than
Eurasian Buzzard,
with longer wings and
tail*

*Usually pale below
with dark patch on
belly. Pale breast
band. Wing-tips and
carpal joints black.
White tail with broad,
dark terminal band*

*Often hovers at low
level when hunting.
Sometimes hunts
from a perch*

The **Rough-legged Buzzard** *Buteo lagopus* (known as the Rough-legged Hawk in the US) is a bird of the northern tundra, where it preys on small mammals, such as lemmings and voles, and some birds. It breeds around the sub-arctic, from Scandinavia, across the USSR (south to Sakhalin on the Pacific coast) and northern North America to Newfoundland. Nesting is in open woodland, scrub and tundra, with eggs being laid from late May to mid-June.

Rough-legged Buzzards migrate far south of their breeding range for the winter, visiting a broad area across Central Europe, Asia and the US. Numbers of migrants to different areas vary greatly from year to year, responding to prey densities.

127

True buzzards and *Buteo* hawks

The pale phase Long-legged Buzzard is shown left

Long-legged Buzzard
Status: *Local*
Length: *50-65 cm*
Wingspan: *135 cm*
The dark phase is shown right

The Long-legged Buzzard's tail is longer than that of Eurasian Buzzard

Orange-brown underwing coverts and body

Upland Buzzard
Status: *Local*
Length: *50-66 cm*
Wingspan: *140 cm*
Similar to previous, but larger and usually less rufous. Also has more heavily feathered legs and darker thighs

The Long-legged Buzzard *Buteo rufinus* is a bird of dry steppes and semi-deserts. It is found in north Africa (especially Morocco), Turkey, Iran and Soviet Central Asia, with a few outposts in Greece, the Middle East and the Arabian Peninsula. In the Balkans, where there are thought to be fewer than 100 pairs, the species occupies a different habitat – low mountain country and wooded hills. Its varied diet includes mammals, reptiles, amphibians, birds and insects, which it hunts by circling or hovering around 30 m above the ground.

The Upland Buzzard *Buteo hemilasius* breeds in the highlands of Central Asia, south to southern Tibet and is sometimes considered as a race of the previous species, which it closely resembles.

Augur Buzzard
Status: *Common*
Length: *50-57 cm*
Wingspan: *130 cm*

Slate-grey above with chestnut-red tail. Augur Buzzard (right and above) is entirely white below, while Jackal Buzzard (far right) is black with chestnut chest. Capable of soaring steadily in strong and variable winds

The Augur Buzzard *Buteo rufofuscus* is one of the most frequently spotted African raptors. It occurs in various habitats from Zimbabwe to Ethiopia, and is particularly common in the east African highlands. In southern Africa, the darker form of this bird (known as the Jackal Buzzard) prevails. It feeds mainly on rodents, including rats and mice.

Red-necked Buzzard
Status: *Locally common*
Length: *44 cm*
Wingspan: *100 cm*
Tail chestnut with black subterminal bar

The Red-necked Buzzard (African Red-tailed Buzzard) *Buteo auguralis* is commonest in tropical west Africa, but is also found in wooded areas and open country in Sudan, Ethiopia and north-west Uganda. It includes small mammals, reptiles and insects in its diet. This bird is one of the smallest African buzzards. It has a distinctive plumage, the orange chest contrasting sharply with the otherwise pale underparts. The Red-necked Buzzard is migratory in the northern part of its range.

In flight, long wings and short tail are visible

Black Solitary Eagle
Status: *Rare/local*
Length: *60-66 cm*
Wingspan: *150 cm*
Dark plumage.
Larger and heavier
than black hawks (p.
106). Short crest

Crowned Solitary Eagle
Status: *Rare/local*
Length: *63-69 cm*
Wingspan: *158 cm*
Grey-brown plumage.
Long wings and short
tail

In flight, it resembles the Black Solitary Eagle

The **Black Solitary Eagle** *Harpyhaliaetus solitarius* is present over a broad area from Mexico in the north, through Central America, south to Ecuador and Peru. In its preferred habitat of forested hills it preys on mammals, snakes and birds.

The Crowned Solitary Eagle *Harpyhaliaetus coronatus* lives in open country and wooded savanna (cerrado) in Brazil, Paraguay, Uruguay, Bolivia and Argentina. Although little is known of its ecology, its prey probably consists of medium-sized mammals, such as skunks. It often perches on posts, and is reputed to be rather tame.

These two impressive eagles are in many ways intermediate between the black hawks and the larger and more powerful harpy eagles. They have similar proportions to the black hawks; and like the harpy eagles, their bills are large and deeply hooked.

New Guinea Harpy Eagle
Status: *Threatened/
narrow endemic*
Length: *75-90 cm*
Wingspan: *150-180 cm*

*Resembles a giant
goshawk. Grey-
brown above, white
below. Long, rounded
tail and short wings.
Facial ruff and erectile
crest*

The New Guinea Harpy Eagle *Harpyopsis novaeguineae* is a native of New Guinea, inhabiting undisturbed forests to altitudes of about 3,000 m. It includes tree kangaroos in its varied diet. In build, it resembles a giant goshawk, and indeed uses goshawk-like techniques to hunt down its prey in the forest interior. It is most often seen soaring above the tree-tops: its broad wings and long rounded tail give it a very distinctive silhouette. It constructs a large nest high up in the forest canopy.

Although still numerous in certain areas, the New Guinea Harpy Eagle is increasingly threatened by hunting (it is highly prized for its feathers) and by habitat destruction. Like other large raptors, it is sensitive to disturbance and is declining rapidly, particularly in lowland forests.

Harpy eagles

Harpy Eagle
Status: *Rare*
Length: *91-110 cm*
Wingspan: *180-220 cm*
Powerful build with large feet and talons. Short, broad wings and long, banded, square-cut tail. Black above, with grey head and neck. White below, with black chest. Facial ruff and divided crest

Short, rounded wings. Long tail. The Harpy Eagle is swift and agile in flight, surprising its prey and grasping it in its massive talons

The **(American) Harpy Eagle** *Harpia harpyja* is widely distributed in the lowland rainforests of Central and South America. It is present from southern Mexico through to northern Argentina, but is rare over most of its range as it is dependent upon unspoiled forest. These birds are difficult to observe since they stay under cover of the dense canopy, hunting in rapid flights from tree to tree.

The Harpy is probably the world's most powerful eagle, as well as one of the largest. It preys on monkeys (especially capuchins) and other forest mammals such as opossums and sloths, as well as birds like macaws. Detection of prey is thought to be aided by its facial ruff, which helps to concentrate and localize sounds (a location system also used by owls).

<u>Guiana Crested Eagle</u>
Status: *Rare*
Length: *79-89 cm*
Wingspan: *158-178 cm*
Similar to Harpy Eagle, but smaller. Common light phase (perched and in flight, above) lacks Harpy's black chest

Banded tail proportionately longer than that of Harpy Eagle. Legs and bill less massive. Prominent single crest. Dark phase (below left) has a black chest and heavy barring below

The Guiana Crested Eagle *Morphnus guianensis* lives in lowland primary rainforest in Central and South America, from Guatemala, Honduras, Costa Rica and Panama, south to Paraguay and northern Argentina. These birds often circle high above the forest canopy, or hunt from a riverside perch. They feed mainly on opossums, monkeys and reptiles.

Both the Guiana Crested Eagle and the Harpy Eagle have very striking plumage, but they are difficult to observe when perched amongst the foliage of the forest canopy. The contrasting plumage patterns break up the birds' outlines against this background, as do the loose head feathers and crest.

Both species build large nests high in the branches of emergent trees. Even in suitable habitats, pairs usually nest several kilometres apart, requiring extensive territories in which to hunt their large prey.

Philippine Eagle

<u>Philippine Eagle</u>
Status: *Endangered*
Length: *86-102 cm*
Wingspan: *185 cm*
*Dark brown above,
off-white below.
Rather untidy crest.
Massive, deep bill*

*A loose mane of long
head feathers is a
characteristic feature
of the adult bird. With
its mottled plumage,
it is well camouflaged
in shady forest*

The Philippine Eagle (Monkey-eating Eagle) *Pithecophaga jefferyi* is
one of the world's rarest raptors, with a population that stands at
about 200. This impressive and powerful bird of prey is now found
only on Mindanao, Luzon (especially in the Sierra Madre mountain
forests), Samar and Leyte. Numbers are still declining, largely because
of habitat destruction, and the species is in imminent danger of
extinction. Captive breeding has been attempted, but without success.
The Philippine Eagle has a slow breeding rate, laying just one egg per
year. It is therefore slow to recolonize suitable habitats.

   This eagle is the Old World counterpart of the Harpy (p. 132). It
usually hunts from a perch, taking mainly monkeys and squirrels, but
also small deer and large birds such as hornbills. It sometimes soars
to a great height and glides down gently over the forest searching for
likely prey, catching it in a final swoop.

Family Accipitridae (part). 31 species in 6 genera

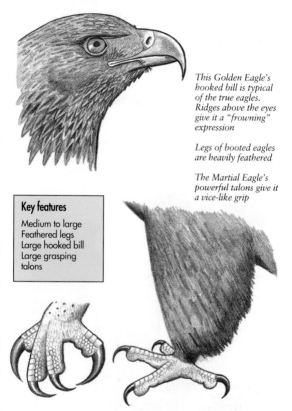

This Golden Eagle's hooked bill is typical of the true eagles. Ridges above the eyes give it a "frowning" expression

Legs of booted eagles are heavily feathered

The Martial Eagle's powerful talons give it a vice-like grip

Key features

Medium to large
Feathered legs
Large hooked bill
Large grasping talons

The booted eagles gained their name from their heavily feathered legs, which, at a distance, can resemble boots. All are large, the majority being shades of brown, black or grey. The sexes are similar, though females tend to be larger than males. Booted eagles feed mainly on live prey, taking a wide range of mammals, reptiles and birds. All but three of the booted eagles fall into three genera: eight are true eagles (*Aquila*) and 20 are hawk-eagles of the genera *Hieraaetus* or *Spizaetus*.

The true eagles have large, powerful bills and prominent ridges over their eyes. The wings are long and rounded, and the legs are feathered to the toes. The Indian Black Eagle, though it resembles the true eagles, has no close relatives and is accordingly classified in a genus of its own.

The seven *Hieraaetus* hawk-eagles are medium-sized birds with feathered thighs, heavy feet and long, sharp claws. Most have a short crest. With the exception of the Black and White Hawk-eagle, all the other hawk-eagles belong to the genus *Spizaetus*. They inhabit tropical forests across the world and are characterized by completely feathered legs, deeply-hooked bills and crests.

This group is completed by. Africa's most powerful eagle – the Martial Eagle – which is sufficiently distinct to be placed in a genus of its own.

True eagles

Both spotted eagles soar on flat wings

Juvenile (above left and perched right) has some whitish spots

Lesser Spotted Eagle
Status: *Local*
Length: *60-65 cm*
Wingspan: *135-160 cm*
Wing-coverts paler than flight feathers

Spotted Eagle
Status: *Local*
Length: *65-72 cm*
Wingspan: *155-182 cm*
Wing-coverts darker than flight feathers. Appears black at a distance

Juvenile (perched far right, in flight far left) has many large whitish spots

The (Greater) Spotted Eagle *Aquila clanga* inhabits forests, particularly those adjacent to wetlands. It is found across most of northern Asia, with a few pairs breeding in eastern Poland and in northern Romania. Birds from the western end of the range winter in east Africa, Turkey and even Italy (Po valley), while eastern birds migrate to northern India and South-East Asia. It takes varied prey from a soaring position, from a perch, or on the ground.

The Lesser Spotted Eagle *Aquila pomarina* has a split distribution, being found in India and north Burma, and reappearing in north-east central Europe, and in east and south-east Europe. Similar in ecology to the Greater Spotted Eagle. Migrates to eastern Africa in the winter.

Pictured in flight:
adult Tawny (far left);
adult Steppe (left);
juvenile Tawny
(below left); juvenile
Steppe (below right)

Both forms soar with
wings held flat or
slightly drooping

Tawny Eagle
Status: Local/
declining
Length: 63-86 cm
Wingspan: 172-260 cm
Brown to cream-
coloured. Long
yellow gape is visible
at close range.
The adult Steppe
Eagle (left) is usually
larger than the adult
Tawny (far left)

Immature Tawny
(right) and Steppe (far
right) Eagles usually
have a white crescent
on the rump and pale
inner primaries, and
often have two pale
wing-bars

The **Tawny Eagle** *Aquila rapax* is a bird of mountains and wooded savanna. It is found in Africa south of the Sahara (though a small, isolated population exists in Morocco), on the dry plains of north and central India, and in Burma. It often steals food from other predators and accompanies vultures at lion kills on the African plains. The Steppe Eagle is a race of the Tawny Eagle, but is sometimes treated as a separate species (*Aquila nipalensis*). It favours open, flat steppes, mountains and semi-deserts. The centre of its population is around the Caspian Sea, where there may be about 5,000 pairs, and east across the Central Asian steppes. Western birds migrate in large flocks to winter in Arabia and north Africa.

Shown here in flight:
adult Spanish bird
(far left); adult
Eurasian birds (left
and below)

Imperial Eagles soar
on flat wings

Imperial Eagle

Status: *Endangered*
Length: *72-83 cm*
Wingspan: *190-210
cm Adult Eurasian (left)
and Spanish (far left)
birds are very dark,
with pale yellow on
head and nape.
Spanish race has pale
shoulders*

The young Imperial
Eagle (right) is similar
to the Tawny and
Steppe Eagles, though
it has more white on
the rump. Full adult
plumage is attained
after five years

In flight, the
immature Imperial
Eagle's streaked and
spotted plumage is
apparent

The Imperial Eagle *Aquila heliaca* ranges from central and south-eastern Europe to the Lake Baikal region of the USSR. There are probably fewer than 1,000 pairs in the USSR (its centre of distribution), while in Europe its numbers have decreased steadily, with less than 100 pairs in Turkey and Romania, 20 pairs in Greece and about 10 pairs in each of Czechoslovakia, Hungary and Bulgaria. The Spanish race, often considered to be a separate species (*Aquila adalberti*), has fared no better, with around 100 pairs remaining in central, western and south-west Spain. Imperial Eagles favour mixed country, with woods and forests alternating with wet areas and grassland. They feed on mammals, birds and reptiles.

Note the long, broad wings with a distinctly curved outline. Adult in flight, left: juvenile, below

Golden Eagle
Status: *Local*
Length: *75-88 cm*
Wingspan: *204-220 cm*
Adult (left) is dark brown with golden neck feathers. Rounded tail

The immature Golden Eagle (right) has white wing-patches and base of tail

The Golden Eagle *Aquila chrysaetos* is found across Europe, north Africa and over much of Asia, to south-east China, Korea and Japan, and in North America (except the eastern US). The British population, which is mainly in Scotland, is probably the largest in Europe, currently standing at about 425 pairs.

Golden Eagles favour highland and mountain country, although lowland populations occur in areas thinly inhabited by people (such as Sweden, Finland and parts of Russia). The largest birds are those in North America and Siberia; the smallest occur near the Mediterranean. Golden Eagles hunt over rocky, open country and along forest edges, for small and medium-sized mammals and birds.

True eagles

Wedge-tailed Eagle
Status: *Locally common*
Length: *89-106 cm*
Wingspan: *250 cm*
Dark plumage. Long, wedge-shaped tail

In flight, adult (above left) and juvenile (above right) show pale wing patches

The immature bird (left) is paler than the adult, particularly on the head and shoulders

The Wedge-tailed Eagle *Aquila audax* is Australia's largest bird of prey, and one of the largest of all eagles. It lives on open plains and in mountain forests, and is often seen gliding and soaring at great height. Wedge-tailed Eagles build huge nests of sticks, lined with eucalypt leaves, usually in tall trees, but occasionally on the ground. Rabbits form an important part of their diet.

Gurney's Eagle
Status: *Unknown*
Length: *76 cm*
Wingspan: *175 cm*
Black above, chocolate brown below. Long, rounded tail

In flight, barring on underside of tail and wings is visible

Gurney's Eagle *Aquila gurneyi* is a species of coastal forest in New Guinea and northern Maluku (the Moluccas). This bird has been little studied, being extremely difficult to observe in its forest habitat. It is threatened by habitat destruction, many coastal forests having been cleared for agriculture.

Verreaux's Eagle has a characteristic flight silhouette, with an S-curve to the hind edge of its wing. Wings held in V when soaring. Whitish wing patch visible in flight

Verreaux's Eagle
Status: *Uncommon and local*
Length: *80-96 cm*
Wingspan: *225-245 cm*
A large, mainly black eagle. White on back and rump. Wings and tail longer than those of Golden Eagle. The immature bird (not shown) is mottled brown

Verreaux's Eagle (African Black Eagle) *Aquila verreauxii* is a large bird found in rocky country in north-eastern and southern Africa. It also occurs in Sinai, and is thought to have bred in Israel. This magnificent eagle is most common in Ethiopia and Kenya, where it breeds mainly on inland cliffs and crags.

Verreaux's Eagle is a specialist feeder, concentrating almost entirely on hyraxes in many areas, but it will also take small antelopes, hares and, occasionally, birds. Pairs indulge in spectacular courtship displays over their breeding territories, typically involving steep climbs and dives, and talon-grappling. These birds usually nest on cliff faces or in tall trees, and raise a single chick to fledgeling.

141

Indian Black Eagle

In flight, the long wings seem to become narrower near the body; this is caused by the bulging secondaries. Adult is shown left. Juvenile (below) is streaked buff-orange below

Indian Black Eagle
Status: *Local*
Length: *65-76 cm*
Wingspan: *180 cm*
Entirely black plumage but for white patches below the eyes and grey upper tail coverts. Head rounded and slightly crested

The Indian Black Eagle has distinctive bright yellow feet. The outer toes are short, and the inner toes have very long claws

The **Indian (Asian) Black Eagle** *Ictinaetus malayensis* is a distinctive bird with no close relatives. Its range takes in Sri Lanka, India, Bangladesh, Burma, south-east China, Taiwan, Malaysia, and much of Indonesia to Sulawesi and Maluku (the Moluccas). It is long, slim and somewhat falcon-like in build and is capable of rapid flight when chasing bats and swiftlets. However, it also feeds by quartering the ground in harrier style, or by flying slowly in the forest canopy and snatching reptiles and birds from amongst the branches.

In slow flight, the Indian Black Eagle splays its long primaries: this prevents stalling and allows the bird to prospect for prey amongst the forest trees in a leisurely fashion. It can sometimes be spotted soaring high above the forest.

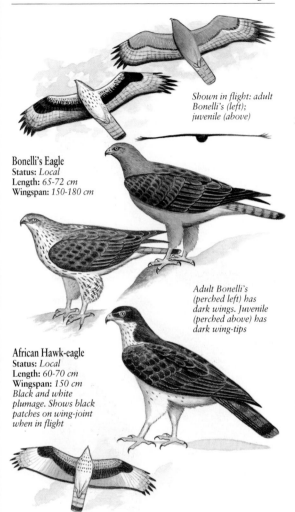

Shown in flight: adult
Bonelli's (left);
juvenile (above)

Bonelli's Eagle
Status: *Local*
Length: *65-72 cm*
Wingspan: *150-180 cm*

Adult Bonelli's
(perched left) has
dark wings. Juvenile
(perched above) has
dark wing-tips

African Hawk-eagle
Status: *Local*
Length: *60-70 cm*
Wingspan: *150 cm*
*Black and white
plumage. Shows black
patches on wing-joint
when in flight*

Bonelli's Eagle *Hieraaetus fasciatus* has a rather scattered breeding range. It is resident in north-west Africa and southern Europe, with strongholds in Morocco and Spain, and also breeds further east, through Iran, India and southern China. The Spanish population is one of the largest – about 400 pairs – but it is threatened and thought to be in decline. Bonelli's Eagle chooses rocky cliffs for nesting, and likes to hunt over maquis and similar scrub, or over adjacent wetlands. It feeds mainly on mammals, birds and reptiles.

The African Hawk-eagle *Hieraaetus spilogaster* frequents wooded savanna and forests in Africa south of the Sahara. Similar to, though smaller than Bonelli's Eagle, it is regarded by some to be a race of that species.

143

Wahlberg's Eagle
Status: *Locally common*
Length: *56 cm*
Wingspan: *128 cm*
A small eagle with long, narrow wings. Long tail

In flight (above), Wahlberg's Eagle could be mistaken for a Black Kite, but for its unforked tail. When perched (right), it shows a distinct crest on the back of its head

Ayres' Hawk-eagle
Status: *Uncommon*
Length: *42-48 cm*
Wingspan: *104 cm*
Spotted below

Chestnut-bellied Hawk-eagle
Status: *Local*
Length: *43-50 cm*
Wingspan: *106 cm*

Wahlberg's Eagle *Hieraaetus wahlbergi* lives in wooded savanna, and along wooded river and lake margins in sub-Saharan Africa. It feeds on gamebirds, small mammals and reptiles.

Ayres' Hawk-eagle *Hieraaetus ayrsii* is a rare forest eagle found in Africa south of the Sahara (especially the highlands of Kenya). It is an agile predator, and often catches its prey, which includes birds and squirrels, in a falcon-like stoop.

The Chestnut-bellied Hawk-eagle *Hieraaetus kienerii* is a forest species found in South-East Asia, Borneo, Hainan, Indonesia (including Sulawesi) and the Philippines. It also breeds in Sri Lanka, south-west India, and the Himalayas.

Shown in flight: light phase (far left); dark phase (left)

Booted Eagle
Status: *Local*
Length: *45-53 cm*
Wingspan: *100-121 cm*
Light phase (right) has dark wings. Dark phase (far right) is all-dark, with pale colour at base of primaries and tail

The **Booted Eagle** *Hieraaetus pennatus* nests mainly in warm, dry woods in hilly country. Spain has the largest European population (around 1,000 pairs), but it also breeds in the USSR, and in a narrow belt east to Manchuria. An isolated population exists in South Africa. Western and northern birds migrate to Africa in the autumn and may be seen in September passing over Gibraltar and the Bosphorus.

Often fans out its tail feathers in flight. The dark phase (shown perched and in flight) has pale areas on the trailing edges of its wings

Little Eagle
Status: *Uncommon*
Length: *45-51 cm*
Wingspan: *120 cm*
Long, feathered legs. Short crest on nape. Like the Booted Eagle, this species occurs in pale and dark phases

The **Little Eagle** *Hieraaetus morphnoides* is found throughout mainland Australia and in eastern New Guinea. Its preferred habitats are scrub and woodland, usually close to water. It has a varied diet that includes large lizards, small and medium-sized birds, small mammals and some insects. Little Eagles build stick nests, little more than half a metre across, high up in trees. In the breeding season, they indulge in high soaring and diving over the nesting site, emitting loud whistling calls.

Black and White Hawk-eagle
Status: *Local*
Length: *50-60 cm*
Wingspan: *110 cm*
Black above, white below. Short crest. Large beak

Black Hawk-eagle
Status: *Local*
Length: *58-66 cm*
Wingspan: *115 cm*

Ornate Hawk-eagle
Status: *Local*
Length: *53-64 cm*
Wingspan: *118 cm*
Long crest. Barred black and chocolate above, white with black bars below

The **Black and White Hawk-eagle** *Spizastur melanoleucus* inhabits lowland rainforests, rivers and clearings in Central and South America, from southern Mexico to southern Brazil. Like the other hawk-eagles, it is a lightly-built bird that preys mainly upon small and medium-sized mammals and birds.

The Black Hawk-eagle *Spizaetus tyrannus* is found in lowland forested habitats from eastern Mexico to northern Argentina and south-east Brazil.

The Ornate Hawk-eagle *Spizaetus ornatus* is another Central and South American species, but is also found in Trinidad and Tobago. It often soars high above the forest canopy and is very vocal, emitting high-pitched screams and whistles.

Changeable Hawk-eagle
Status: *Locally common*
Length: *51-70 cm*
Wingspan: *106-135 cm*

Light form (in flight above, perched right) is brown above, white below with black streaks on throat and chocolate streaks on breast. Dark form is shown in flight (far right)

Mountain Hawk-eagle
Status: *Local*
Length: *62-78 cm*
Wingspan: *121-145 cm*
Chocolate-brown above, rufous below. Long white-tipped crest. Tail has dark brown barring

Streaking on upper breast only. Belly barred. Tail bands broader than in the Changeable Hawk-eagle

The **Changeable Hawk-eagle (Crested Hawk-eagle)** *Spizaetus cirrhatus* has a wide distribution, overlapping all the other Asian hawk-eagles except the Sulawesi Hawk-eagle. It is found in India and the Himalaya, Sri Lanka, Bangladesh, Malaysia, Indonesia, Borneo and the Philippines. This raptor favours forests, especially those with frequent clearings, and it is often associated with villages. There are many geographical variations in plumage.

The **Mountain Hawk-eagle (Hodgson's Hawk-eagle)** *Spizaetus nipalensis* is found in South-East Asia, south-east China, Hainan, Taiwan, Japan, the Himalaya, and also in western India and Sri Lanka. It lives mostly in mountain forests during the breeding season, but may move down to lower levels in winter.

147

Blyth's Hawk-eagle
Status: *Local*
Length: *48-53 cm*
Wingspan: *86-105 cm*
Smaller than Changeable Hawk-eagle

Blyth's Hawk-eagle is very dark above. Belly and thighs are barred black and white. Tail is white with wide black subterminal band. Long crest

Cassin's Hawk-eagle
Status: *Rare*
Length: *54 cm*
Wingspan: *110 cm*
Dark chocolate-brown and black above, white below

Blyth's Hawk-eagle *Spizaetus alboniger* replaces the Mountain Hawk-eagle in the mountain forests of peninsular Thailand, Malaysia, Sumatra and Borneo. It is variable in plumage, some forms being almost entirely black beneath. Immature birds are dark brown above, with pale heads and buff-coloured underparts. These birds emit characteristic loud, piercing calls.

Cassin's Hawk-eagle *Spizaetus africanus* is a rarely-seen species that inhabits the dense forests of west and central Africa. It is known from Kayonza forest in south-west Uganda. This species, one of only three *Spizaetus* eagles in Africa, has been little studied, partly because its habitat is very inaccessible. It occurs with the Crowned Eagle (p.152) and the Long-tailed Hawk (p.103), competing for food with both of these species.

Hawk-eagles

Strongly barred beneath, with a darker belly than the Changeable Hawk-eagle

Javan Hawk-eagle
Status: *Endangered*
Length: *54 cm*
Wingspan: *110 cm*
Belly brown with whitish bars. Distinct crest

Sulawesi Hawk-eagle
Status: *Local*
Length: *54 cm*
Wingspan: *110 cm*
Belly and thighs barred chocolate and white. Short crest

Strongly barred underparts. Ringed tail. Belly paler than that of the Javan Hawk-eagle

The **Javan Hawk-eagle** *Spizaetus bartelsi* is endemic to the forests of Java, where it is now found only in a few reserves. Though this bird was once widespread on the island, its population may now be as low as 60 pairs, most of the remaining birds being found on the eastern side of Java. It favours forests on the low slopes, commonly between 200 and 1,200 m up.

The **Sulawesi Hawk-eagle** *Spizaetus lanceolatus* is restricted to Sulawesi and the surrounding islands. It is found in both lowland and highland forests, to about 1,500 m, and is often spotted as it sails over the trees. It is very similar in plumage to the Barred Honey Buzzard (p. 21), with which it overlaps: this is thought to be an example of mimicry. These hawk-eagles build their nests high in the branches of tall forest trees.

Hawk-eagles

Tht Phillipine Hawk-eagle is rufous below, with heavy streaking

Phillipine Hawk-eagle
Status: *Rare*
Length: *60 cm*
Wingspan: *122 cm*
Black and chocolate-brown above. Underparts rufous with black streaks on chest

Wallace's Hawk-eagle
Status: *Rare*
Length: *45 cm*
Wingspan: *90 cm*
Light rufous below, with a black-barred belly. Tail has three broad, black bands

Similar in appearance to Blyth's Hawk-eagle (p. 148), but note the banded tail

The **Philippine Hawk-eagle** *Spizaetus philippensis* is a rare forest eagle found only on certain islands in the Philippines group (including Luzon, Mindoro, Palawan and Negros).

Wallace's Hawk-eagle *Spizaetus nanus* is the smallest of the hawk-eagles. It is found in south Burma, south Thailand, Malaysia, Borneo and Sumatra, where it is thinly spread in lowland forest, and threatened by habitat loss. In the field, immature birds cannot reliably be separated from young Blyth's Hawk-eagles.

In common with many forest raptors, populations of both the above birds have declined in recent decades with the continued felling of lowland forests.

When in flight, the Long-crested Eagle displays white patches on the undersides of its wings

Long-crested Eagle
Status: *Locally common*
Length: *51-56 cm*
Wingspan: *116 cm*
Blackish-brown plumage. Long, rather floppy crest. Long wings and short tail. Talons are small for the bird's size

The Long-crested Eagle *Spizaetus occipitalis* inhabits open country and wooded areas in sub-Saharan Africa. It feeds mainly on rodents and may often be seen keeping watch from a prominent perch, such as a telegraph pole. Long-crested Eagles sometimes breed in inhabited areas, even in towns. They are buzzard-like in general behaviour, soaring over open scrub and grassland while prospecting for prey.

Isidor's Eagle
Status: *Uncommon*
Length: *64-74 cm*
Wingspan: *152 cm*
Glossy black above, chestnut below. Tail pale grey with a broad terminal black band. Long black crest

Isidor's Eagle displays a striking brown, black and white pattern beneath

Isidor's Eagle (Black and Chestnut Eagle) *Spizaetus isidori* is found at high altitudes in the northern and central Andes, from Venezuela to north-west Argentina. It prefers to nest on east-facing slopes of forested gorges, at altitudes of about 2,000 m. It preys mainly on monkeys, squirrels and other medium-sized mammals, but will also take birds. These birds typically nest in tall trees near cliffs or rocky valleys. Females lay just a single egg each season.

Crowned Eagle
Status: *Uncommon*
Length: *81-91 cm*
Wingspan: *135-154 cm*
Rounded halo-like crest

The Crowned Eagle has rounded wings. Its flight silhouette is like that of a giant sparrowhawk

The Crowned Eagle *Spizaetus coronatus* lives in the highland forests of central and eastern Africa, especially Kenya and Zaire. In build, it resembles a sparrowhawk, presumably a similar adaptation to flying and hunting within a wooded habitat. It is slightly less bulky, but more powerful than the Martial Eagle and concentrates mainly on mammalian prey, taking small antelopes, hyrax and monkeys. These eagles usually rear a single chick each season, making use of the same stick nest year after year.

Martial Eagle
Status: *Local*
Length: *76-86 cm*
Wingspan: *155-187 cm*
Rounded crest. Dark brown above. Breast and belly white, with dark spots

The white belly of the Martial Eagle contrasts sharply with its brown wings

The Martial Eagle *Polemaetus bellicosus* occurs in savanna, and along forested rivers in East Africa. Its territory is always large, with an average size of 130 square km. It preys on birds such as guineafowl and francolins, but will also take mammals, especially monkeys, small antelopes and hyrax. This powerful bird hunts from a great height, using its acute vision to detect prey below. It is often seen perched atop an *Acacia* tree or soaring high above hilltops.

152

Falcons

Family Falconidae (part). 38 species in 1 genus

This Peregrine shows the large eye and sharp, notched bill typical of the falcons

A falcon's foot has long, thin toes and sharp claws

Key features

Small to medium
Long pointed wings
Long tail, often tapered
Bill deeply hooked, with notched upper mandible
Small head
Large eye, often surrounded by bare skin
Sexes similar
Females larger

The Hobby has a swift-like silhouette

With their sleek, streamlined shape, dashing flight and ferocious predatory behaviour, falcons epitomize birds of prey. They are found in all continents, from tropical regions right up into the high arctic. The members of this group range in size from the compact Merlin and American Kestrel (sometimes confusingly called Sparrowhawk) to the bulky Gyr Falcon. Correspondingly, the prey taken ranges from insects and small birds in the smallest species, to game birds and mammals up to the size of hares, in the larger falcons.

These birds have long, pointed wings and strong, sharply hooked bills, of which the upper mandibles are distinctly notched. Their vision is acute, and the eyes are large in relation to body size. Many species of falcon have a distinct moustache-like marking on the face. Plumage is usually dark above and pale beneath, with the sexes being similar in appearance, though the female is usually larger and bolder than the male. They usually lay four or five buff-white, speckled eggs per season: these are incubated for about 30 days.

All falcons are built according to the same basic body plan, and their similarity of shape and body structure is reflected in their close taxonomic relationship, all the world's falcons being classified in the single genus *Falco*. Falcons do not build nests, but use either a ledge or hollow in a tree, or take over existing nests of other species. Females are preferred for the sport of falconry. In most species of kestrel, however, the sexes are dissimilar.

In flight, the adult female (left) shows heavily streaked underparts. Note the short outer tail feathers (both sexes)

The adult male (right) shows pale orange breast and spotted belly in flight

American Kestrel
Status: *Common*
Length: *25 cm*
Wingspan: *50-60 cm*
"False eyes" on nape are thought to deter predators. The adult male is shown left

The adult female (right) differs from the male in having a red-brown back and tail, barred with black. Juveniles (not shown) are similar to adults, though the immature male has a white, streaked breast

The **American Kestrel** (**Sparrowhawk**) *Falco sparverius* is found throughout almost the entire American continent, from southern Canada and the USA, through central America and the Caribbean, to Tierra del Fuego. However, it is notably absent from much of Amazonia. It favours open country, grassland, desert, woodland margins and meadows, but is occasionally seen in urban areas.

This bird is the only North American falcon which regularly hunts by hovering. Rodents, insects, small birds, and reptiles are all a regular part of its diet. The sexes differ in plumage. American Kestrels usually nest in holes in trees, but they will also make use of nest boxes, barns and other buildings.

Shown here in flight: adult female (top left); adult male (centre and bottom left)

Kestrels hover before dropping on to their prey

Long, pointed wings and very long tail are visible in flight

Kestrel
Status: *Common*
Length: *32-35 cm*
Wingspan: *71-80 cm*
The adult male is shown right

The sexes differ in plumage. The adult female (left) is brown, heavily spotted and streaked. The male has a blue-grey head and tail

The Kestrel *Falco tinnunculus* is arguably the most numerous bird of prey in the world. It is certainly Europe's commonest raptor and also occurs in Africa (except the Sahara and Congo basin) and most of Asia (except the extreme north and south-east). This bird is often seen perched on a telephone wire, or hovering expertly over rough ground, such as a roadside verge. Through agile movements of its wings and tail, the kestrel can keep its head absolutely still while hovering: this allows it to focus clearly on the ground below and spot its prey – chiefly small rodents. Kestrels normally nest in holes in trees. They lay a clutch of between three and six eggs, which the female incubates for about four weeks.

Kestrels

The male (in flight, left and below) has brighter plumage than the Kestrel

Lesser Kestrels appear slender and graceful in flight. Wings are pointed at tips

Lesser Kestrel
Status: *Threatened/ declining*
Length: *29-32 cm*
Wingspan: *58-72 cm*
Slimmer in build than the Kestrel, with narrower wings and tail. Shown left is the adult male

The adult female (right) differs from the male in that it has a spotted back (although the sub-adult male has spots). Both sexes are paler than in the Kestrel

The Lesser Kestrel *Falco naumanni* of southern Europe, north-west Africa and south and central Asia is a smaller and more delicate version of the Kestrel. It has strongholds in Portugal and Spain (where it is still locally common, but decreasing) and about 1,000 pairs are resident in Morocco. It is a colonial breeder, nesting in groups of up to 200 pairs, in cliffs or caves, or on buildings in towns and villages. Lesser Kestrels rely mainly on large insects, such as grasshoppers and beetles, for food. The use of agricultural pesticides has reduced the availability of this prey and caused a decline in numbers. These raptors are migratory, overwintering in parts of southern Africa, particularly Botswana, Namibia and South Africa.

The Greater Kestrel has a blue-grey rump, and a black-barred tail

Greater Kestrel
Status: *Local*
Length: *36 cm*
Wingspan: *80 cm*
Sexes similar in appearance; both resemble the female European Kestrel. Creamy-white eye

Fox Kestrel
Status: *Local*
Length: *38 cm*
Wingspan: *86 cm*

Sexes similar in appearance. Copper coloured plumage with black streaks

Flight feathers are black. Long wings. Long, graduated tail accounts for over half of the bird's length

The Greater Kestrel (White-eyed Kestrel) *Falco rupicoloides* is found in open bush country in southern and eastern Africa, north to Somalia and Ethiopia. It is common in many parts of Botswana and southern Zambia, where it breeds in the abandoned nests of other species, such as crows. It occasionally hovers to watch for prey in the grass below, but prefers to hunt from a perch.

The Fox Kestrel *Falco alopex* is the world's largest kestrel. It is restricted to a belt of inland Africa to the south of the Sahara, where it nests on cliffs. Known from the Turkana district of northern Kenya.

Underside of wings faintly barred. Yellow face with bare skin

Grey Kestrel
Status: *Local/ uncommon*
Length: *36 cm*
Wingspan: *81 cm*
Sexes similar

Dickinson's Kestrel
Status: *Local*
Length: *32 cm*
Wingspan: *72 cm*
Sexes similar. Both have grey plumage

Blackish back and greyish-white rump. Tail is strongly barred and has a wide black terminal band

The Grey Kestrel *Falco ardosiaceus* is found in western and central Africa, north to Sudan and Ethiopia, and south to southern Tanzania. This bird favours wooded and cultivated areas close to water, and is most active around dawn and dusk, feeding mainly on other birds, lizards and large insects, but also on bats. It takes over and breeds in abandoned nests of Hammerkops (stork relatives).

Dickinson's Kestrel *Falco dickinsoni* is another grey kestrel. It favours woodland in southern Africa (though it is absent from the Cape region). Like the Red-headed Falcon (p. 170), it likes to nest in the tall *Borassus* palms typical of low-lying wet savannas. Local in Tanzania (including Pemba Island). Often attracted to grass fires.

Black flight feathers. Hovers before dropping onto prey

In flight: adult female (above); adult male (right)

Australian Kestrel
Status: *Common*
Length: *30-36 cm*
Wingspan: *75 cm*

Male (perched above) has grey head and tail. Female is shown perched right

Moluccan Kestrel
Status: *Common*
Length: *28-30 cm*
Wingspan: *66 cm*

Resembles European Kestrel, but more rust-coloured

The **Australian Kestrel** (**Nankeen Kestrel**) *Falco cenchroides* is Australia's commonest bird of prey. It lives mainly in open plains in Australia, Tasmania and parts of New Guinea, but is also found in coastal dune habitats and sometimes on farms, in gardens and cities. Like the European Kestrel (p. 155), it is frequently seen hovering at the roadside. It may occur in large numbers during rodent or locust plagues. Australian Kestrels nest in hollow trees, or on ledges of cliffs or buildings.

The **Moluccan Kestrel** *Falco moluccensis* lives in Java, Maluku (the Moluccas) and in Sulawesi and nearby islands. It is very similar to the European Kestrel in both plumage and behaviour.

Kestrels

Note the slightly pointed blue tail of the pale phase bird

Madagascar Kestrel
Status: *Local/narrow endemic*
Length: *26 cm*
Wingspan: *58 cm*
Rich chestnut above, pale below. Dark phase (not shown) has chestnut breast

Madagascar Banded Kestrel
Status: *Local/narrow endemic*
Length: *29 cm*
Wingspan: *64 cm*
Grey above. Grey face and breast

Black tail. Barred black and white below

The Madagascar Kestrel *Falco newtoni* and the Madagascar Banded Kestrel (Barred Kestrel) *Falco zoniventris* are both found in Madagascar, although the former also occurs in the Comores Islands, which lie to the north-west of Madagascar and in Aldabra (in the Seychelles group).

The Madagascar Kestrel is tame and approachable. It takes a wide range of prey, including lizards, rodents and large insects. Immature birds closely resemble young European Kestrels (p.155); however the latter species does not occur on Madagascar.

The Madagascar Banded Kestrel frequently nests amongst epiphytes in the branches of trees, but little is known about its biology.

In flight, the Mauritius Kestrel shows its rather short, rounded wings and pale belly with white spots

Mauritius Kestrel
Status: *Endangered/ narrow endemic*
Length: *24 cm*
Wingspan: *48 cm*
Sexes similar. White below, with large heart-shaped spots. Relatively short, rounded wings

Seychelles Kestrel
Status: *Narrow endemic*
Length: *22 cm*
Wingspan: *45 cm*
Relatively short, rounded wings

The Seychelles Kestrel frequently soars in circles over its territory

The **Mauritius Kestrel** *Falco punctatus* is one of the world's rarest birds of prey, found only in certain tracts of forest in the south-west of the island of Mauritius. Only a handful of breeding pairs have been recorded. This species has been the subject of a captive breeding and release programme, aimed at increasing the wild population, and now showing signs of success. It feeds mainly on geckos.

The **Seychelles Kestrel** *Falco araea* is the smallest true falcon and is found only in the Seychelles.

Both of the above falcons have short, rounded wings, rather similar in shape to those of the sparrowhawks. This is an adaptation to hunting in the confines of forest interiors.

Merlin

The banded tail tail of the female (far right and below left) is obvious in flight. The male is shown in flight right and below right

In outline, the Merlin resembles a tiny Peregrine, with a broad base to the wing

Merlin
Status: Local/declining
Length: 25-30 cm
Wingspan: 50-62 cm
The male bird (right) is slate-blue above, white or brown below, with dark streaks

The female Merlin (left) is grey-brown above, with a bold pattern of streaks and blotches on the pale breast and belly

The Merlin (Pigeon Hawk) *Falco columbarius* is a small, active falcon, which specializes in catching small birds in surpise low-level attacks. It is found in northern Europe (including Iceland and the British Isles), across northern Asia and northern North America. In Scandinavia, Merlins breed mainly in birch thickets, but in Britain the preferred habitat is high-growth heather moor. In Canada, Merlins even breed in some towns and cities, such as Saskatoon, where House Sparrows make up the bulk of their diet. Most Merlins migrate south for the winter, though in some parts of the range (Iceland, Britain, Ireland and Scandinavia), they stay near their breeding grounds throughout the year. Wintering birds often feed near the coast.

The Eurasian Hobby's long, narrow wings give it a swift-like silhouette

In flight, the Eurasian Hobby uses shallow wing-beats, interspersed with swoops and glides. It rarely hovers

Eurasian Hobby
Status: *Local*
Length: *30-36 cm*
Wingspan: *82-92 cm*
Slate-coloured above. Rufous thighs. Clear moustache. The long wings extend well down towards the tip of the tail when the bird is perched

The Eurasian Hobby (Northern Hobby) *Falco subbuteo* is a graceful and active predator of flying insects and small birds. It breeds in much of Europe, north to southern Britain and southern Scandinavia, north-west Africa, and across Asia to Kamchatka, northern Japan and south-east China. Favoured habitats are heathland with scattered trees, or open forest. Hobbies are summer visitors, wintering in southern Africa, India and South-East Asia.

They often feed in the evening, on large insects such as cockchafers or dragonflies, or on small birds gathering to roost. Birds are caught in the air in a burst of fast, agile flight. Hobbies can even catch swallows and swifts in this way.

163

Hobbies

Rufous below, not just on thighs

African Hobby
Status: *Local*
Length: *28-31 cm*
Wingspan: *75-80 cm*
Smaller and more brightly coloured than Eurasian Hobby

Oriental Hobby
Status: *Local*
Length: *25 cm*
Wingspan: *65 cm*
Cheeks entirely black. Dark grey above, chestnut below (including wings)

Australian Hobby
Status: *Uncommon*
Length: *35 cm*
Wingspan: *90 cm*
Slate-blue to blackish above. Rufous below, with blackish streaks. Note the dark cheek and pale patch on the side of the neck, which extends to form a half-collar

The African Hobby *Falco cuvieri* lives along forest edges and in wooded savanna in central, eastern and southern Africa.

The Oriental Hobby *Falco severus* is found in south-east China, South-East Asia, Hainan, Philippines, Java, Sumatra, Borneo, Sulawesi, New Guinea and Solomon Islands. Its preferred habitat is woodland and it includes bats in its diet.

The Australian Hobby (Little Falcon) *Falco longipennis* is the smallest Australian falcon. It is also found in New Britain, Maluku (the Moluccas) and Lesser Sunda Islands. Like other hobbies it has a swift-like flight and feeds mainly on birds and insects. It is occasionally seen over city parks and gardens.

Slightly smaller than Hobby. Flight feathers pale. Frequently hovers

Shown in flight: adult male (above); adult female (right)

Red-footed Falcon
Status: *Local*
Length: *30 cm*
Wingspan: *66-78 cm*
The adult male is shown left

The adult female (right) is yellow or rusty below, blue-grey and barred above

Amur Falcon
Status: *Local*
Length: *30 cm*
Wingspan: *70 cm*
Adult male (left) has chestnut lower belly, thighs and under tail coverts

In flight, white lower wing coverts are obvious. Male right, female far right

The (Western) Red-footed Falcon *Falco vespertinus* is distributed from eastern Europe, through the western and central Soviet Union, east to the upper Lena river. In Europe it occurs mainly in Hungary (about 600 pairs) and Romania (about 120 pairs). It favours grasslands and wooded steppes, river valleys and marshes, and feeds mainly on insects, although the young are also fed vertebrates. Red-footed falcons usually nest in colonies and migrate to southern Africa in the autumn.

The Amur Falcon (Eastern or Manchurian Red-footed Falcon) *Falco amurensis* is a close relative of the Red-footed Falcon. It is found in north-east Asia, where it lives in open country, and migrates to southern China, India and South-East Asia.

Other falcons

Shown in flight: adult light phase (far left); dark phase (left)

Sooty Falcon
Status: *Very local*
Length: *33-36 cm*
Wingspan: *85-110 cm*
Adult light phase (perched right); dark phase (far right). Cere and feet yellow

The Sooty Falcon *Falco concolor* is a desert species found scattered in the Arabian peninsula, Egypt, Libya, Sudan and Ethiopia (Red Sea coast). It occasionally breeds in Israel. This migrant species winters mainly in Africa, Madagascar and on Indian Ocean islands. Like Eleonora's Falcon, it feeds largely on migrant birds at its breeding sites, and on large insects in winter. Sooty falcons usually breed in colonies of up to 100 pairs. They lay a clutch of two to four eggs on a ledge on a cliff or in a cave.

Eleonora's Falcon
Status: *Very local*
Length: *36-40 cm*
Wingspan: *110-130 cm*
Larger than Hobby

Adult pale phase is cream to red brown below, dark above. Dark phase is slate grey all over, with paler flight feathers

Eleonora's Falcon *Falco eleonorae* is one of the world's most graceful falcons. About 5,000 pairs are scattered throughout the Mediterranean (with a stronghold in the Greek islands), on the Morroccan coast and in the Canaries. It breeds in colonies of between 5 and 200 pairs, mainly on island cliffs, in July and August (later than any other European bird), and feeds its young on nocturnally-migrating birds. Its winter quarters are in East Africa and the Indian Ocean islands.

Flight feathers pale below. Soars with wings swept upwards

Brown Falcon
Status: *Common*
Length: *40-51 cm*
Wingspan: *96 cm*
The pale phase birds shown here have a double moustache

New Zealand Falcon
Status: *Local/ declining*
Length: *37 cm*
Wingspan: *75 cm*
Very dark above, with pale feather edges. Streaked below. Rufous thighs

In flight, the New Zealand Falcon's wings appear short and rounded

The Brown Falcon *Falco berigora* (also known as the Cackling Hawk or Chicken Hawk) is a common Australian raptor, and probably the noisiest, often uttering hen-like cackling or piercing screeches. It lives in a wide range of habitats, from mountain forests to open plains, farms and coastal dunes. Brown Falcons are variable in plumage, with dark, pale and intermediate phases occurring. The dark phase is uniformly dark brown, but pale beneath the wings.

The New Zealand Falcon *Falco novaeseelandiae* is primarily a forest species, with a rather sparrowhawk-like build. This species is threatened by habitat destruction, and is now restricted to highland forests and offshore islands.

Other falcons

The Black Falcon has broad wings, which are slightly drooped when soaring

Black Falcon
Status: *Uncommon*
Length: *48-56 cm*
Wingspan: *98 cm*
Larger and more robust than the Brown Falcon

Grey Falcon
Status: *Local/rare*
Length: *33-43 cm*
Wingspan: *90 cm*
Cere, eye-ring and legs yellow. Underwings pale grey with dark tips

The juvenile Grey Falcon (right) is darker than the adult, with streaking below

In flight, the Grey Falcon's wings appear markedly tapered. The adult is shown left

The Black Falcon *Falco subniger* is a rather uncommon falcon found in the dry interior of Australia. It favours plains, grasslands, watercourses, and agricultural areas. Black Falcons feed primarily on small and medium-sized birds, often caught near rivers or waterholes. They breed in old crows' nests, laying a clutch of two to four eggs each breeding season.

The Grey Falcon *Falco hypoleucos* is found in dry *Acacia* scrub and tussock grassland in Australia, but is seen only rarely. It flies using shallow, flickering wingbeats. This bird has declined markedly over recent years, and contracted in range, probably due to pressures on its habitat from agriculture.

The Bat Falcon is dark and closely-barred beneath, except for its pure white chin

Bat Falcon
Status: *Local*
Length: *24-30 cm*
Wingspan: *55-70 cm*
Similar to Orange-breasted Falcon, with less chestnut on chest

The Bat Falcon *Falco rufigularis* is distributed throughout Central and South America (east of the Andes), from southern Mexico to northern Argentina, where it favours damp, tropical lowland forest. As its name suggests, it preys on bats, which it catches in the air. However, like most other falcons, it also takes small birds, including fast-flying species such as swifts and hummingbirds. It is similar in plumage to the larger Orange-breasted Falcon, but its habits are quite different.

Orange-breasted Falcon
Status: *Rare/local*
Length: *33-40 cm*
Wingspan: *76-92 cm*
Slate-blue above, dark orange below, with black barring on chest. Resembles the Bat Falcon, but is larger and heavier

The Orange-breasted Falcon has the silhouette and flight action of a Peregrine

The Orange-breasted Falcon *Falco deiroleucus* has a similar range to the Bat Falcon, though it is a far rarer bird. Its favoured habitat is lowland forest and savanna woodland, and it feeds mainly on birds, such as doves and parrots. Although this species hunts over lowland forests, it breeds at somewhat higher altitudes (up to about 1,500 m). This bird is the ecol[g]cal equivalent of the Peregrine (p.174), which is absent from most of South America.

Other falcons

The Red-headed Falcon is barred black and white below

Red-headed Falcon
Status: *Local*
Length: *30-36 cm*
Wingspan: *70-83 cm*
Grey and thick-set in appearance. Chestnut cap

Taita Falcon
Status: *Rare*
Length: *36-41 cm*
Wingspan: *84-96 cm*
Resembles a small, dumpy Lanner Falcon (p. 172), but tail shorter. Grey-white rump

The Taita Falcon is reddish beneath, with streaks on the belly

The Red-headed Falcon (Merlin) *Falco chicquera* is found in India (not Sri Lanka) and Africa, where it is commonest in southern Sudan and northern Uganda, and in coconut plantations along the East African coast. It usually nests in *Borassus* and Doum palms, although it breeds in scrub in the Kalahari Desert, and feeds mainly on birds.

The Taita Falcon *Falco fasciinucha* is a rare species from east and central Africa. It is most common in south-west Ethiopia and Kenya, especially in the Tsavo and Amboseli National Parks. It is also known from the Zambezi Gorge (Victoria Falls) on the Zambia/Zimbabwe border. The bird is named after Kenya's Taita Hills where it was first described.

The Aplomado Falcon's long, pointed wings and banded tail are visible when the bird is in flight

Aplomado Falcon
Status: *Local/ uncommon*
Length: *35-45 cm*
Wingspan: *78-102 cm*
Grey crown. Dark patches on sides of chest. Breast and belly cinnamon

Prairie Falcon
Status: *Local*
Length: *37-47 cm*
Wingspan: *90-113 cm*
Uniformly pale. Narrow moustache. Large eye and dark ear-patch

The Prairie Falcon has distinctive dark patches on the undersides of its wings

The **Aplomado Falcon** *Falco femoralis* inhabits light forest, open country, desert and dry grassland in Mexico, Central and South America. Now extinct as breeding species in the US, it is being reintroduced from captive-bred stock in southern Texas. It feeds mainly on birds, which it usually takes in rapid forays from a perch.

The Prairie Falcon *Falco mexicanus* is found in dry, open country in the western half of North America, from southern Canada to northern Mexico. These falcons usually nest on cliffs and hunt their mammal and bird prey in open country, either from the air or from a look-out post. Ground squirrels are a favourite prey. They are similar in ecology and appearance to Asian Saker Falcons (p. 172).

Other falcons

Lanner Falcon
Status: *Local/rare*
Length: *34-50 cm*
Wingspan: *90-115 cm*
Slender build

Pale grey above, pale buff below. Rufous on crown and nape

Lagger Falcon
Status: *Locally common*
Length: *34-50 cm*
Wingspan: *90-110 cm*

Grey-brown above. Streaked belly

Saker Falcon
Status: *Local/rare*
Length: *45-55 cm*
Wingspan: *102-126 cm*
Pale head

Brown above, pale below. Spotted belly

The Lanner Falcon *Falco biarmicus* is scattered throughout Africa and the Arabian peninsula, and also occurs in Italy and the eastern Mediterranean. It favours rocky country with cliffs and open dry savanna and scrub, and preys mostly on small and medium-sized birds.

The Laggar Falcon *Falco jugger* is the commonest large falcon in northern India. It favous dry open plains and mountain foothills.

The Saker Falcon *Falco cherrug* is found in China and central Asia, with about 150 breeding pairs in eastern Europe. This powerful steppe and desert falcon feeds mainly on ground-living mammals, but also takes birds. It winters in the Mediterranean, Caucasus, Middle East and East Africa, and is much prized by falconers.

Shown in flight: adult dark (top), white (centre) and intermediate grey (bottom) phases

The Gyr Falcon has long wings, which are broad at the base, and rounded at the tips

Gyr Falcon
Status: *Uncommon*
Length: *50-60 cm*
Wingspan: *110-160 cm*
White (right), dark (far right) and intermediate grey (below) phases occur. Dark phase is grey above, white below with dark spots. White phase is almost pure white, with black wing tips

Gyr Falcons are buzzard-sized birds with large heads. Long belly feathers may cover the feet when perched. In the grey phase, spots on the underside merge into barring along the flanks

The Gyr Falcon *Falco rusticolus* is the largest of all the falcons. It is a bird of arctic tundra, rocky coasts and northern mountain country, and has a circumpolar distribution that takes in Greenland, Iceland, northern Scandinavia and the Soviet Union, as well as Alaska and northern Canada. These birds normally hunt by chasing their prey (birds such as grouse and waterfowl, and mammals including hares) in rapid, low-level flight. Birds from Greenland occasionally reach western Europe (especially Ireland and Britain). Gyr Falcons have long been regarded as the finest birds for falconry, which poses a potential threat to their numbers in the wild. However, populations currently appear to be stable.

Other falcons

In flight, the Peregrine's long, pointed wings are visible. Tail short. Underside is pale and often banded

Peregrine
Status: *Vulnerable*
Length: *35-50 cm*
Wingspan: *94-116 cm*
Dark head and broad moustache contrast with white cheeks. Adult shown right. Juvenile (far right) is yellowish below

Barbary Falcon
Status: *Local*
Length: *34-40 cm*
Wingspan: *80-100 cm*
Resembles Peregrine, but slimmer in build. Juvenile is shown above left, adult below left and in flight

Crown and nape red-brown. Moustache not as conspicuous as Peregrine's.

The Peregrine (Falcon) *Falco peregrinus* is found on all continents except Antarctica, though it is rare over much of its range. In North America, it occurs mostly in the Arctic areas of Alaska and Canada. In South America, it is present only on the southern tip, and it is absent from the Sahara region, the Arabian peninsula and central Asia. Its European strongholds are Spain (about 2,000 pairs) and Britain and Ireland (around 1,000 pairs). The Peregrine catches birds, often in a spectacular gravity-assisted dive, with its wings closed. Activities of gamekeepers, egg-collectors and falconers have reduced its numbers.

The Barbary Falcon *Falco pelegrinoides* inhabits arid areas in north Africa, the Arabian peninsula, Iran and parts of central Asia.

Pygmy falcons and falconets. Forest falcons

Family Falconidae (part). 14 species in 4 genera

Pygmy falcons, like this African Pygmy Falcon, have all the features of falcons in miniature

Key features

Very small
Notched bill
Long wings
and tail

Forest falcons raise their head feathers to form a ruff, which may help to detect sound

Key features

Wings short and rounded
Long, rounded tail
Facial ruff
Barred below

The pygmy falcons and falconets are tiny, falcon-like birds which feed largely on insects. They behave rather like shrikes, making short sallies from a prominent perch to capture their prey. There are just two species of pygmy falcon, one found in Africa, the other in South-East Asia. All six falconet species are South-East Asian; five are closely related and grouped in the same genus. They include the world's smallest bird of prey, the Bornean Falconet, in their number. These birds resemble miniature falcons, with notched bills, and long wings and tails.

Forest falcons are small birds adapted to hunting lizards, small birds and invertebrates amongst the dense foliage of Central and South American tropical rainforests. They show some convergent features with the sparrowhawks, including short, rounded wings, long tails and barred undersides. Several also have a distinct facial ruff.

Pygmy falcons

Shown in flight:
female (far left); male
(left). Note brown
back of female

African Pygmy Falcon
Status: *Local*
Length: *22 cm*
Wingspan: *34 cm*
*Perches prominently
on thorn bushes.
Adult male (right);
female (far right)*

White-rumped Pygmy Falcon
Status: *Local/
uncommon*
Length: *25 cm*
Wingspan: *40 cm*
*White rump and
underparts. Male
(perched) has grey
head and nape with
black streaks. Female
(head detail) has
chestnut head*

*Tail more graduated
than in the falconets*

The **African Pygmy Falcon** *Polihierax semitorquatus* is a tiny falcon with shrike-like appearance and habits. It lives in dry bush and savanna in eastern and southern Africa, and is locally common in parts of northern Kenya, especially near the nests of Buffalo Weavers, in which it breeds. This bird hunts flying insects in flycatcher-like aerial forays, and also takes small reptiles and birds. It is easily spotted, spending long periods perched on exposed branches.

The **White-rumped Pygmy Falcon** (Fielden's Falconet) *Polihierax insignis* inhabits dry, open woodland in South-East Asia and Burma, to about 900 m. It feeds mainly on insects, but also catches small birds, snakes and frogs.

The Spot-winged Falconet is parrot-like both in outline, and in its clambering behaviour

Spot-winged Falconet
Status: *Local/narrow endemic*
Length: *28 cm*
Wingspan: *45 cm*
Rather drab olive-brown in colour. Streaked plumage. White rump

Pied Falconet
Status: *Locally common*
Length: *19 cm*
Wingspan: *33 cm*
Very small. Similar to Collared Falconet (p. 178), but lacks white collar. Black ear-patch. White below

In flight, the Pied Falconet shows pale wings and belly, and a barred tail

The Spot-winged Falconet *Spiziapteryx circumcinctus* is an unusual species not closely related to the other falconets. It is relatively large and lives in open woodland on the pampas of northern Argentina. Its ecology has been little studied, but it is thought to feed mainly on small birds and mammals.

The Pied Falconet *Microhierax melanoleucus* is a bird of woodland and open areas in south-east China, Assam, and South-East Asia. It is found at altitudes of up to 900 m. This is the largest member of the genus and it is capable of killing small mammals, birds and reptiles, though insects make up a large part of its diet. It frequently nests in trees, in old woodpecker holes.

177

Pale wings contrast with rufous chin and thighs. The tail is distinctly barred

Collared Falconet
Status: *Widespread*
Length: *19 cm*
Wingspan: *30 cm*
Very small. Black and white forehead and black mask. White below. Rufous throat, thighs, flanks and under tail coverts

Black-thighed Falconet
Status: *Local*
Length: *15 cm*
Wingspan: *26 cm*
Lacks white collar

A diminutive bird. Black ear-patch. Black sides and thighs. White or light rufous below

The **Collared Falconet (Red-legged Falconet)** *Microhierax caerulescens* is found at altitudes of up to 2,800 m in the northern and eastern Himalayan foothills, in Burma (to about 1,800 m), and in South-East Asia. This bird of open forest and forest margins hunts mainly for insects, which it takes in flycatcher-style forays. It also preys on small and medium-sized birds, even species larger than itself, such as thrushes. It nests in old woodpecker and Barbet holes.

The **Black-thighed Falconet** *Microhierax fringillarius* inhabits forest edges and secondary forests to about 1,200 m in peninsular Thailand, Malaya, Sumatra and Java. It occasionally builds its nests in the roofs of houses.

Dark wings and tail contrast sharply with white body

Philippine Falconet
Status: *Local*
Length: *19 cm*
Wingspan: *33 cm*
Diminutive in stature. Greenish black plumage above. White throat, breast and belly

Bornean Falconet
Status: *Local/narrow endemic*
Length: *15 cm*
Wingspan: *25 cm*
Diminutive in stature. White crown and black mask.

The Bornean Falconet has a dark tail and thighs, but pale breast and wings

The **Philippine Falconet** *Microhierax erythrogonys* is only found on islands in the Philippines. Its includes butterflies and moths in its diet. Like the other species of this genus, The Philippine falconet is tiny in stature. It has a beautiful greenish gloss to its black plumage; this together with its streamlined shape gives it the appearance of a martin, especially when in flight. It relies on rapid, darting flight to capture its prey.

The **Bornean Falconet** *Microhierax latifrons* is the world's smallest bird of prey, weighing only about 35 g. It inhabits forest to about 1,500 m in north-east Borneo and Sabah, and is said to be particularly partial to dragonflies.

Forest falcons

The grey phase Barred Forest Falcon (perched below right; in flight, right) occurs in Mexico. Both phases are closely barred on underside

Barred Forest Falcon
Status: *Common*
Length: *35 cm*
Wingspan: *50 cm*
Plumage varies according to location. Red phase (perched far left; in flight, above right) occurs in Brazil and Paraguay

Lined Forest Falcon
Status: *Local*
Length: *33 cm*
Wingspan: *47 cm*
Grey above, pale below with grey barring

Collared Falcon
Status: *Common*
Length: *50 cm*
Wingspan: *70 cm*
White collar. Long black and white-barred tail. Pale (far left) and orange-breasted (left) phases occur

The **Barred Forest Falcon** *Micrastur ruficollis* has a wide range that stretches from southern Mexico, through Central America, to Paraguay and northern Argentina. It feeds on small birds, reptiles and rodents, and has been known to follow army ant trails to locate small insectivorous birds that feed on the ants.

The **Lined Forest Falcon** *Micrastur gilvicollis* is a little-known species found in the dense rainforest of the Amazon basin.

The **Collared Forest Falcon** *Micrastur semitorquatus* has a similar range to the Barred Forest Falcon. It favours dense forest up to about 2,500 m, where it takes a wide range of prey.

Note the single tail band

Plumbeous Forest Falcon
Status: *Rare/local*
Length: *32 cm*
Wingspan: *46 cm*
Similar to Barred Forest Falcon (p. 180)

Slaty-backed Forest Falcon
Status: *Rare*
Length: *39 cm*
Wingspan: *55 cm*
*Slate-grey above.
Similar to Collared Forest Falcon*

Traylor's Forest Falcon
Status: *Rare/local*
Length: *39 cm*
Wingspan: *53 cm*
Similar to Collared Forest Falcon

The **Plumbeous Forest Falcon** (**Sclater's Forest Falcon**) *Micrastur plumbeus* lives in the wet forests of south-west Colombia and north-west Ecuador, at altitudes of between about 600 and 900 m.

The **Slaty-backed Forest Falcon** *Micrastur mirandollei* is a rare species of lowland rainforest, found from the northern Amazon region, north to Panama and Costa Rica. It is more widely distributed than the Plumbeous and Traylor's Forest Falcons, and shares most of its range with the Barred and Collared Forest Falcons.

Traylor's Forest Falcon *Micrastur buckleyi* is known only from a few specimens collected in Ecuador and north-east Peru.

Laughing Falcon

Family Falconidae. 1 species in 1 genus

When in flight, the
Laughing Falcon
displays its short,
broad wings and
long, fan-shaped tail.
It is seldom seen in
the air, spending long
periods perched in the
forest

Laughing Falcon
Status: *Widespread*
Length: *45 cm*
Wingspan: *65 cm*
*Chunky build. Large
head, with slight
crest. Claws are
razor-sharp.
Upperparts chocolate,
head and underparts
sandy white. Black
mask. Tail is black,
though lower tail is
barred white*

The **Laughing Falcon** *Herpetotheres cachinnans* is a tree-top snake-hunter found in the tropical forests of Central and South America. Its range stretches from southern Mexico to northern Argentina, and includes all the rainforests of Amazonia. It also occurs in thorny scrub in more arid areas.

The Laughing Falcon takes its name from its unique laughing alarm call and loud song. Pairs of birds sing duets at dawn and dusk, based on a repeated "wah-co" "wah-co" call. Otherwise they can be difficult to locate since they are sit-and-wait predators. They eat poisonous as well as harmless snakes, first removing the venom by biting off the snake's head. Occasionally seen soaring above the forest canopy.

Family Falconidae (part). 9 species in 4 genera

Key features

Large-sized
Naked face
Deep bill
Long legs with flat
claws
Mainly dark

*This Crested
Caracara shows the
heavy bill and patch
of bare skin typical of
the group*

*Caracaras spend
much time on the
ground, hopping amd
walking on their long
legs, which have flat
claws*

*In flight a caracara's
silhouette is crow-like*

Caracaras are large, scavenging birds restricted to Central and South America. Although related to the falcons, they are very different both in habits and appearance. Like the vultures, they have heavy bills and areas of naked skin on their faces, adaptations associated with feeding on carrion. They also include insects and, unusually for birds of prey, plant matter, in their diet. These birds occasionally kill for themselves, but habitually pirate food from other raptors, even vultures, harassing them until they disgorge their crop contents.

Caracaras have an efficient flapping flight, but do not soar in thermals as often as vultures. They also spend much time on the ground, walking well on their flat toes. Their wings are wide and rounded, and they have long necks and legs; the sexes are similar in plumage. Caracaras build nests of sticks, usually sited on a cliff or in a tree. They lay two or three eggs, which both sexes incubate for about 32 days.

The largest genus, *Phalcoboenus*, comprises four species of dark, crow-like raptors of mountain country and shorelines in South America. However, the Crested Caracara, the largest and most widespread of the caracaras (just reaching North America), is classified in its own genus. The two species of the genus *Daptrius* are found in rainforests of Amazonia and Central America.

The wings of the Crested Caracara have whitish patches and are held slightly crooked and arched downwards in flight

In flight, the Crested Caracara appears black, with a white patch at each extremity (head and tail as well as wing tips). The long, thick neck is also distinctive

Crested Caracara
Status: *Locally common*
Length: *54-60 cm*
Wingspan: *118-132 cm*
Blackish-brown in overall colour. Throat and neck are white. Large head, long neck. Facial skin is red. Bill is heavy and deep. Also note the crest on the back of the head

The Crested (Common) Caracara *Polyborus plancus* is the only member of its genus. It is a common scavenger in most parts of South and Central America, and also frequent in southern Texas, central Florida and southern Arizona. Its preferred habitat is open scrub, such as prairie, savanna and pampas.

Crested Caracaras are generalist hunters, catching and killing small mammals, birds, fish, amphibians, reptiles and invertebrates. They also steal food from other raptors, such as Black and Turkey vultures, and are sometimes seen patrolling roads on the lookout for fresh corpses. They are slow and deliberate in flight and frequently soar when searching for prey.

The Red-throated Caracara has glossy black plumage. In flight, its long, rounded tail is visible

Red-throated Caracara
Status: *Locally common*
Length: *48-53 cm*
Wingspan: *106-117 cm*
Beak yellow, cere grey. Bare reddish skin on throat. Feet and legs red

Yellow-throated Caracara
Status: *Local*
Length: *43-48 cm*
Wingspan: *95-106 cm*
Beak black, cere yellow. Bare yellow skin on throat. Feet yellow

Glossy black plumage, with white base to tail. Tail shorter and less rounded than that of the Red-throated Caracara

The **Red-throated Caracara** *Daptrius americanus* and the Yellow-throated (Black) Caracara *Daptrius ater* are birds of deep tropical forests. The former has a range that extends from southern Mexico, through Central America, to southern Brazil, whilst the slightly smaller Yellow-throated Caracara is restricted to the Amazon basin.

Unlike most other birds of prey these caracaras include a lot of fruit in their diet, though they also feed on insects. They have known to open up the nests of wasps (even those with powerful stings) and feast on the nutritious grubs inside. Red-throated Caracaras are noisy birds which can often be spotted flying in small groups over the forest canopy, uttering loud cackling calls.

185

Caracaras

Heavy streaks on the Carunculated Caracara's belly are cleary visible in flight

Carunculated Caracara
Status: *Local*
Length: *51-56 cm*
Wingspan: *112-123 cm*
Wattled throat. Dark belly with white streaks. Short, curly crest along the top of the head

Mountain Caracara
Status: *Widespread*
Length: *48-53 cm*
Wingspan: *106-117 cm*
Glossy black above and on chest. White wing-coverts, belly and thighs. Notice the modest bill of this generalist feeder

All-black chest distinguishes the Mountain Caracara from the above species. Long legs

The Carunculated Caracara *Phalcoboenus carunculatus* is found in the Andean uplands of south-west Colombia and Ecuador. It is more sociable than the other members of its genus, and may sometimes be seen in groups of up to 50 birds.

The Mountain Caracara *Phalcoboenus megalopterus* replaces the previous species in the central Andes, from Ecuador, Peru and Bolivia, to northern Chile and Argentina. It frequents mountain country, usually above 1,000 m, where it is a familiar scavenger around farms and villages. In parts of Chile, however, it can be seen at sea-level. Mountain Caracaras feed on carrion, worms, insects, and sometimes small mammals and birds.

The White-throated Caracara is the only species of this group to show an all-white body in flight

White-throated Caracara
Status: *Local*
Length: *48-53 cm*
Wingspan: *106-117 cm*
Throat and underparts white. White tip to tail

Striated Caracara
Status: *Local*
Length: *53-58 cm*
Wingspan: *117-128 cm*
Dark plumage, with white streaks on neck and breast. Chestnut thighs. Larger and heavier than the other members of the genus

In flight, the Striated Caracara shows white wing-patches and white tip to tail

The **White-throated Caracara** *Phalcoboenus albogularis* inhabits Andean slopes and woodland. It is particularly common in the extensive Southern Beech (*Nothofagus*) forests of southern South America (especially the Patagonia region of southern Argentina).

The Striated Caracara (Forster's Caracara) *Phalcoboenus australis* is restricted to the Falkland Islands and islands off Tierra del Fuego. It is essentially a shoreline scavenger, preying upon young and weak seabirds and penguins, carrion and insects. Striated Caracaras breed amongst rocks, constructing a very simple nest of twigs, grass and animal hair (sometimes including sheep's wool). Two or three eggs are laid each season.

The Yellow-headed Caracara is mostly sandy-brown below, with dark brown on the trailing edge of the wings and tip of the tail

Yellow-headed Caracara
Status: *Common*
Length: *41-46 cm*
Wingspan: *90-101 cm*
Slightly larger than the Chimango Caracara. Head, neck and underparts sandy. Wings dark brown. Black line behind eye

Chimango Caracara
Status: *Locally common*
Length: *38-43 cm*
Wingspan: *84-95 cm*
Reddish brown above. Cinnamon below, with barring

The rufous colouring of the Chimango Caracara is visible in flight, as is the fine barring on the tail

The **Yellow-headed Caracara** *Milvago chimachima* is found east of the Andes, from Panama to northern Argentina, and is one of the commonest birds of prey in this region. It is often seen in small groups.

The **Chimango Caracara** *Milvago chimango* is most common on the pampas of Argentina, but may be seen in suitable open country throughout South America, south of Brazil. It also occurs on the Falkland Islands. It is a sociable bird that sometimes follows the plough, like seagulls and crows.

Both of the above caracaras, and those of the genus *Phalcoboenus*, behave like crows, and are their ecological equivalents in South America. They sometimes perch on livestock to pick off ticks.

Index of latin names

Index of latin names

Index of common names

Index of common names